EMBROIDERY DESIGNS
FROM PRE-COLUMBIAN ART

Books by Barbara L. Snook

Embroidery Designs from Pre-Columbian Art

Florentine Embroidery

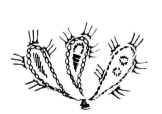

EMBROIDERY DESIGNS FROM PRE-COLUMBIAN ART

by Barbara L. Snook

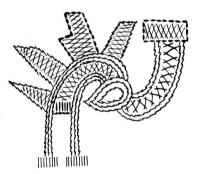

Charles Scribner's Sons · New York

THIS BOOK PUBLISHED SIMULTANEOUSLY IN
THE UNITED STATES OF AMERICA AND IN CANADA—
COPYRIGHT UNDER THE BERNE CONVENTION

1 3 5 7 9 11 13 15 17 19 MD/C 20 18 16 14 12 10 8 6 4 2

PRINTED IN THE UNITED STATES OF AMERICA
Library of Congress Catalog Card Number 73–2552
ISBN 684–13988–X

ACKNOWLEDGMENTS

A long time ago, in 1930, my design tutor, Mrs. Anne Gasston, in her lectures on world ornament, made me aware of Pre-Columbian art. For this and much else there is to her a permanent debt of gratitude. Not until 1950, after a year in the U.S.A. could I visit Mexico and then had to wait until 1968 before a journey to Peru could be organized. On my way via New York, my friends Mrs. Joan Toggitt and Miss Margot Rosenmund suggested that a book might be the outcome, if not the purpose of the trip. The idea soon became important and my sincere thanks are given for their enthusiasm. On my return, quite by chance and with great good fortune, I met Mr. William Kaplan to whom is offered an especial "Thank you" for he enabled me to see, behind the scenes, part of the collection being prepared by Mr. Orsin Riley, whose help is also gratefully acknowledged, for the exhibition later held at the Guggenheim Museum, and which I should otherwise have missed because it opened after my return to England. My thanks are due too, to the staff at the Textile Museum, Washington, D.C., and to Mrs. Elizabeth Leonard, Curatorial Assistant, and Mr. Milton Sonday, Assistant Curator then at the Cooper Union Museum, New York. My visits are inevitably rare but on every occasion the help given by each branch of the Textile Museum has been enormous and unstinting. Scribner's Art Department deserves much admiration and thanks for so competently handling a very difficult manuscript, and once again my sincere gratitude to my editor Elinor Parker for her readiness to offer, from her great experience, all manner of practical advice and above all for her encouragement.

CONTENTS

INTRODUCTION

Aztec, Maya, Inca, names to fire the imagination and lure travellers to strange lands; names associated with mythological gods, part man, part serpent, part jaguar; legends and cults mystifying and remote. Enthralled by stories of the Aztec Quetzelcoatl, the Mayan "Sacred well" and jungle-entwined pyramids, the Incas' "Lost City" and astounding treasure destroyed by Spanish conquistadores, we may forget the artistic achievement of the earliest craftsmen working 2000 years before Inca goldsmiths cast their spell upon us.

In selecting design material for embroidery from the Pre-Columbian civilizations, Peru and its neighbors, Colombia and Bolivia, have proved the most fertile source of ideas. The monumental character of Aztec and Mayan art makes adaptation to embroidery difficult, thus comparatively few examples from these two cultures have been used.

Peru is a country divided geographically into three regions, a vast, formidable coastal desert; the Alti Plano, a high inland plain; and the tropical forest only now being penetrated by archaeologists. Whether coastal or highland, each locality and era produced work of marked individuality. Chavin, Wari, Mochica, Tiahuanacan and Paracas craftsmen were endowed with such a pronounced sense of pattern and command of both strong and subtle color that today their work steadily increases in popularity.

This highly developed pattern sense is shown in all their work, much of which is symbolic, impossible for the layman to understand, sometimes difficult to disentangle when component parts, birds, serpents and men spring from one another, sharing heads or dividing into two as the case may be. Apparently abstract patterns, too, may, even on closer study, be found to contain curiously involved human-animal-bird forms, while interlocking designs of creatures moving forever in both directions are commonplace.

The absolute dryness of the coastal desert has preserved, in burial shrouds, unique fabrics, and it is said that almost all the weaving techniques known today were discovered and used by the Paracas weavers. They created gauzes, nets, double and triple cloths, brocades and tapestry weaves. Printed fabrics and embroidery were less important. Few stitches were used, satin, double running, darning, closed herring-bone, long-armed cross, surface buttonhole, and most common of all, varieties of stem. These I have actually seen but know that further study may reveal more.

Garish colors make today's Sunday markets a brilliant spectacle, though it is sad to see the detrimental effect of recent dyes supplanting the age-old tradition of handling natural dyestuffs. Unexpectedly perhaps to all but modern craftsmen-dyers, the old range was wider and much more exciting. Often the actual number of colors in one piece of work is deceptive, but their movement through a design is so cunningly contrived, linked with an instinctive feeling for the bright use of contrasting light and dark tones, that a color check can reveal a surprisingly low total count. We may have to blend many more shades to attain a comparable result.

Pre-Columbian craftsmanship is well represented in museums in Central and South America, the U.S.A., and Europe. Many excellently illustrated books have been published, indeed there is no shortage of information for those unable to go far from home. Even nowadays, with Mexico, Yucatan, Colombia, Bolivia and Peru more accessible than once upon a time, they still present enough problems and surprises to deter the less intrepid traveller.

KEY TO STITCHES / For diagrams see Index of Stitches.

Back ----	French knot
Buttonhole ⊔⊔⊔ closed	Gobelin
Chain ∞∞∞ detached	Greek cross
rosette twisted	Half chevron
Coral knot	Herringbone XXX closed XXXXXX
Couching	back-stitched XXXXX
Cretan	Parisian
Cross X X double or Smyrna ✳✳	Rice
interlaced	Ringed-back
long armed	Roumanian
Darning	Satin counted
Dot	Seeding
Double knot	Sprat's Head
Double running	Star ✳ ✳ ✳
Eyelets	Stem
Feather	encroaching
long-armed	Portuguese knotted
Fern	Tent ////// reversed \\\\
Fishbone	Tufting
Florentine diagonal	Web spider
Fly couched	Wheatear, detached
Four-sided	Wheatsheaf

LAMPSHADE/Birds and Animals

FABRIC	White open-weave linen, 24 threads to the inch
THREAD	White stranded cotton
STITCHES	Counted satin, eyelets; the tails are small pompoms sewn on when embroidery is finished.
SOURCES OF DESIGN	Horned animal from a Paracas printed fabric, in the museum, Cuzco; llama and bird, woven textiles, Lima
OTHER USES	Cushions, table linen, dress decoration
HOW TO MAKE	See page 4.

Changes in angle of beak

The tail is part of
a back-stitched eyelet.

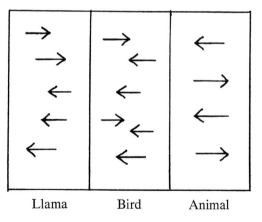

Llama   Bird   Animal

The frame is in six sections.
Work two of each design.

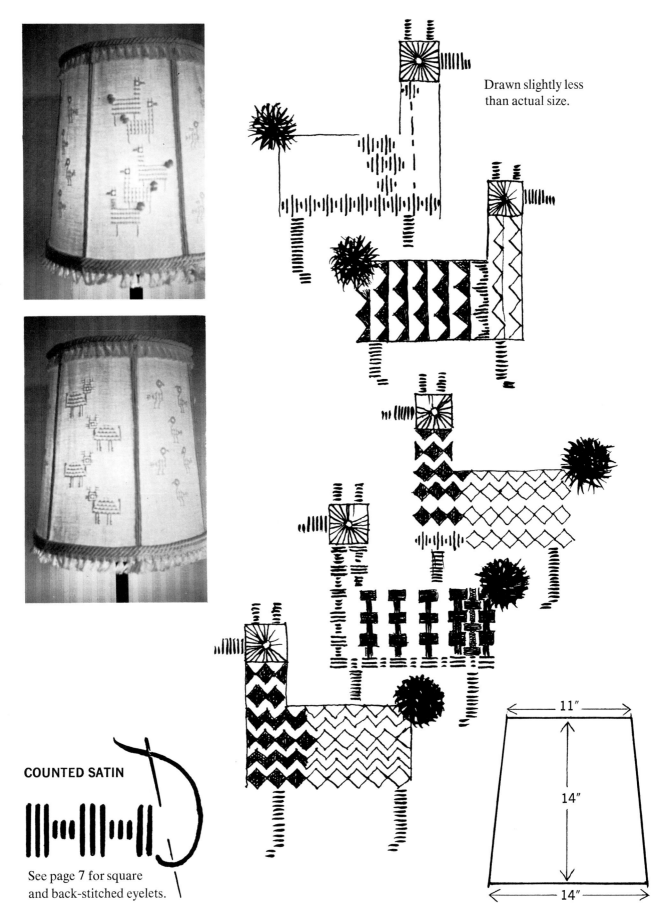

Drawn slightly less than actual size.

COUNTED SATIN

See page **7** for square and back-stitched eyelets.

11"

14"

14"

3

LAMPSHADE/Snake's Head

FABRIC	White open-weave linen
THREAD	White stranded cotton
STITCHES	Counted satin, diagonal chained border
SOURCE OF DESIGN	Chancay textile, Lima
OTHER USES	a. On table linen, runners, and place mats
	b. For canvas work
	c. As border on beach robe or bathrobe
	d. On upholstery tweed to enrich cushions matching a suite
	e. Vertically as room divider on open weave, 18 to 22 threads to the inch

These shades are almost cylindrical; therefore, the material is cut straight on the thread and the first two are worked on the counted thread. When the embroidery is complete the bottom edge is machine stitched to the white lining, opened out, pressed, and the edges tacked ready for the long seam to be stitched. After turning to the right side the material is pulled over the frame, from the bottom upward, taking care not to twist the seam. The top is pinned, easing in any slight fullness, tacked, and neatly oversewn. The appearance of both edges is improved by the addition of a fringe.

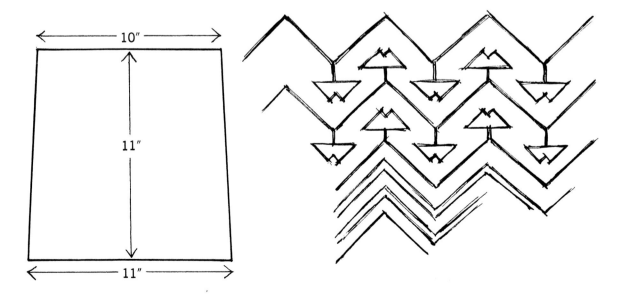

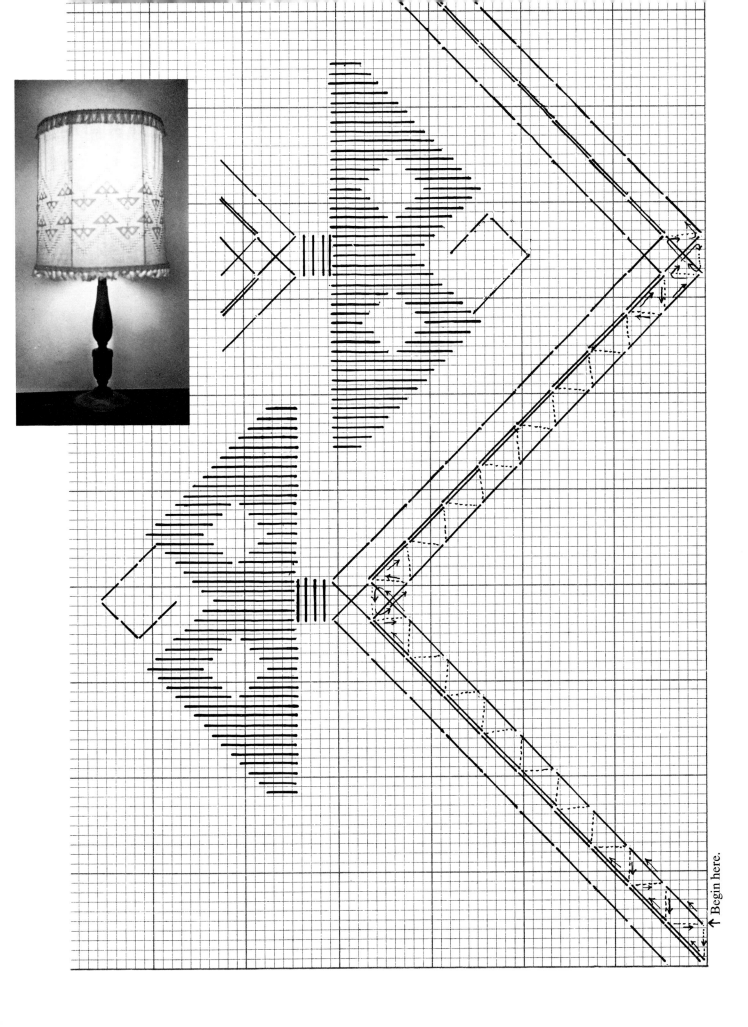

Begin here.

Place mats and runner

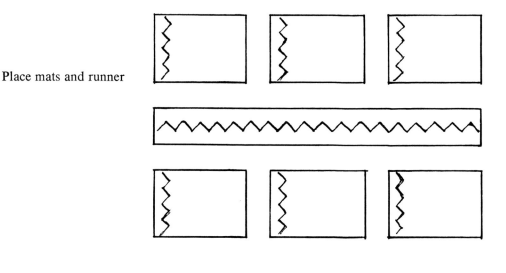

Wall hanging

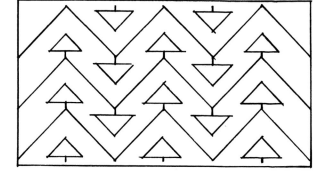

DIAGONAL CHAINED BORDER

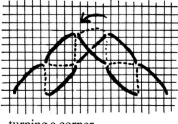

turning a corner

Pattern of snake's head
used for hemmed appliqué

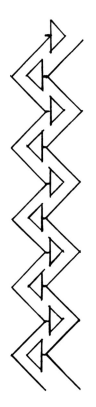

DIAGONAL CHAINED BORDER

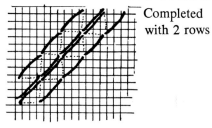

 Completed
with 2 rows

LAMPSHADE/Beans

SEE PLATE 3.

FABRIC	Open-weave linen
THREAD	Stranded, soft cotton, crewel, 3-ply knitting wool
COLOR	Shades of yellow, greenish yellow, gold, ochre, and white
STITCHES	Back, chain, detached chain, couching, eyelets, stem, seeding, Roumanian, buttonhole wheel
SOURCE OF DESIGN	Colored beams in diagonal rows, embroidered with alpaca wool on cotton fabric, Early Nazca, Peru
OTHER USES	a. With gold kid and beads for evening bag
	b. A belt
	c. Curtain border
	d. Canvas work upholstery
HOW TO MAKE	See page 4.

The lampshade frame has six divisions. The row of embroidered beans which fit into each section do not hide the metal support; this is covered by couching, a vertical line of color which helps to strengthen the design.

The original fabric was worked entirely in encroaching stem stitch.

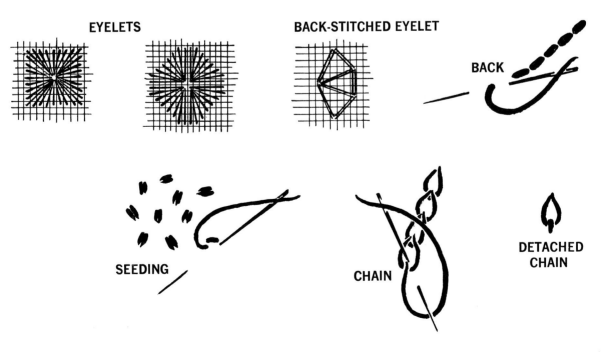

EYELETS   BACK-STITCHED EYELET   BACK

SEEDING   CHAIN   DETACHED CHAIN

8

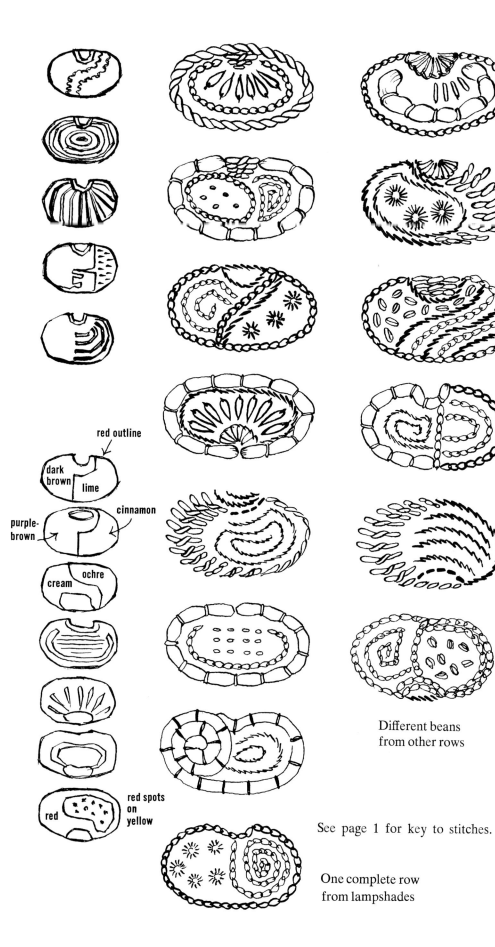

red outline

dark brown

lime

purple-brown

cinnamon

ochre

cream

red

red spots on yellow

Different beans from other rows

See page 1 for key to stitches.

One complete row from lampshades

FURTHER SUGGESTIONS

Gold kid and beads for evening purse

or belt, one or two rows

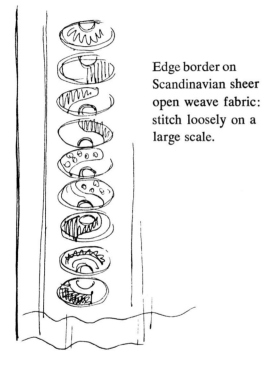

Edge border on Scandinavian sheer open weave fabric: stitch loosely on a large scale.

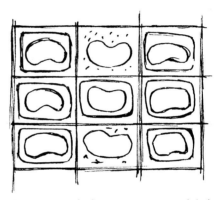

Pattern variations as seen on fabrics from the Museum of Primitive Art, New York (above) and the Textile Museum, Washington (below).

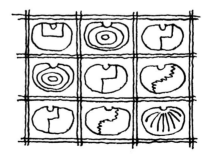

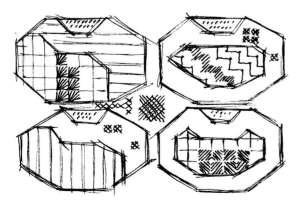

Canvas — all over design

SHALLOW HANGING LAMPSHADE
diameter 8 inches

FABRIC	Stiff white bridal satin
THREAD	White pearl cotton No. 5 and No. 8
STITCHES	Coral knot, closed herringbone, fly, satin, stem, encroaching stem, Portuguese knotted stem, straight
SOURCE OF DESIGN	A painted vase, possibly Mochica, Peru
OTHER USES	a. Border on child's shirt b. Ends of evening sash
HOW TO MAKE	The embroidery for this shade was supported by two 8″ separate wire rings, one plain, the other made with the light bulb fitting. These were held apart by buckram oversewn to them. The underside of the shade was covered with a circle of bridal satin matching the embroidered band and machined to it. This was pinned in place, the top turned in a very small hem, folded over the top ring and sewn to the buckram invisibly.

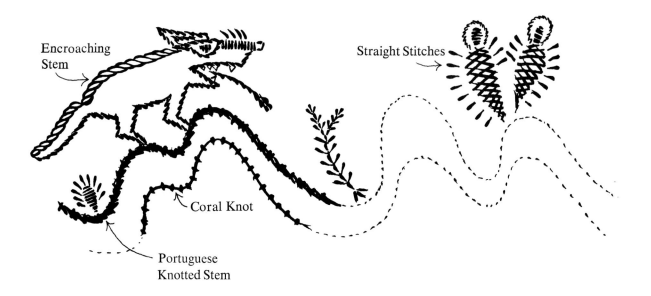

Encroaching Stem

Straight Stitches

Coral Knot

Portuguese Knotted Stem

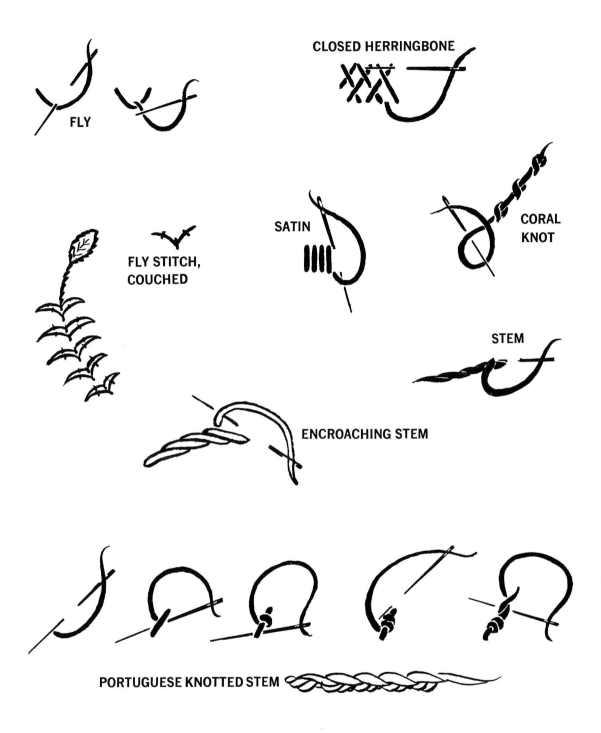

FLY

CLOSED HERRINGBONE

FLY STITCH, COUCHED

SATIN

CORAL KNOT

STEM

ENCROACHING STEM

PORTUGUESE KNOTTED STEM

NOTE   When making a shallow lampshade which encloses the bulb it is necessary to measure the depth of the bulb and to allow adequate clearance beneath it, otherwise the heat from the bulb will cause the fabric to burn.

LAMP BASE

FABRIC	Orange red upholstery tweed
THREAD	Crewel and tapestry wool, a little pure silk, a few beads
COLOR	Navy, 3 shades turquoise, cerise, 3 shades yellow, salmon, plum, purple
STITCHES	Chain, closed herringbone, couching, cross, double cross, darning, Portuguese knotted stem, rice, Roumanian, satin, stem, wheatsheaf

Sometimes the size of the stitches can be altered to give variety. Different thread thicknesses also help, and a few beads change the texture.

SOURCE OF DESIGN	Poncho-shirt, cotton and wool tapestry, Classic Tiahuanaco, Bolivia
OTHER USES	a. Cushion
	b. Wastepaper basket
	c. Room divider, with the design much enlarged and many more rows of stitches to fill the greater area
HOW TO MAKE	The embroidery covers a can weighted with dry sand. The cord passes between the can and the fabric; the base is not sewn in until the cord is in place. After a piece of balsa wood is cut to fit the cylinder and the lamp fitting, the top is covered with felt.

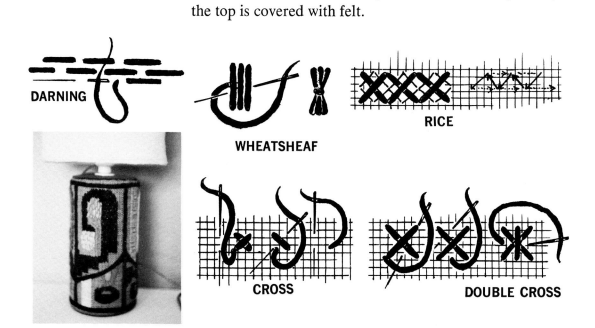

DARNING

WHEATSHEAF

RICE

CROSS

DOUBLE CROSS

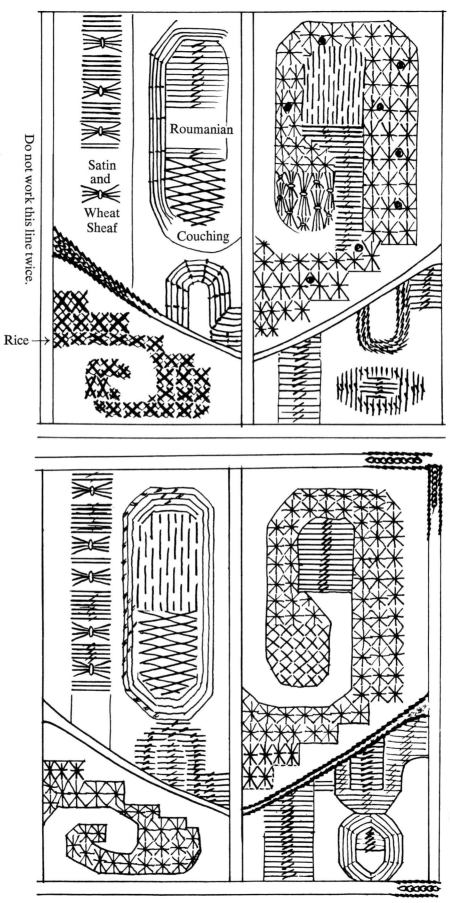

Do not work this line twice.

Satin
and
Wheat
Sheaf

Rice →

Roumanian

Couching

See page 1 for
key to stitches.

HASSOCK/Frog

FABRIC	Furnishing tweed or cotton
THREAD	Crewel wool
COLOR	Tones of fabric and a little contrasting color
STITCHES	Stem, satin, couching, fly, Cretan, Roumanian, double knot, Portuguese knotted stem, Spanish knotted feather
SOURCE OF DESIGN	The frog motif was suggested by the design on a Nazca pot found in the Rafael Larco Herrera Museum, Lima. The colors are fawn, mid-brown, rust red, and white. The design on the bowl-shaped pouf is similar to that on the pottery where the feet join to make a star.
OTHER USES	Top only, a cushion Border, a bag
HOW TO MAKE	Cut paper templates of the frog and move these about on paper until they fit well and make the required size. From this pattern measure the amount of material to buy; the length of the side panel is approximately three times the diameter of the circle. Lay the templates on the fabric and tack round the design. If the top is to be smaller than the base, darts will be needed in the top of the border. It is simpler to make the side vertical and the circle to fit exactly. After the embroidery is finished, machine the seams together leaving an opening on the bottom edge for stuffing. Use something firm such as wood shavings or a synthetic material. Close the seam with tight over-sewing.

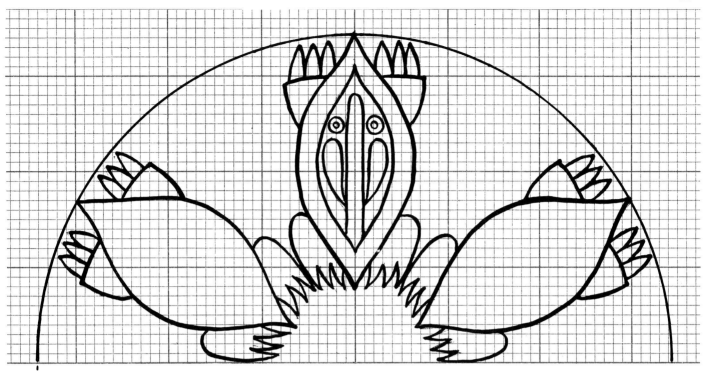

FROG

See page 1 for key to stitches.

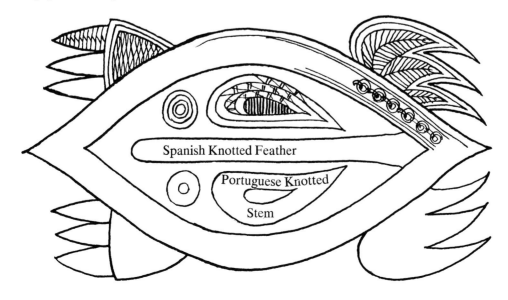

Spanish Knotted Feather

Portuguese Knotted

Stem

CUSHION/Fish

FABRIC	Slub silk, dark moss green
THREAD	Stranded cotton
COLOR	2 shades cream, lime green, pale yellow
STITCHES	Double knot, fern, detached wheatear, stem, chain, couching
SOURCE OF DESIGN	A silver fish sewn on a Peruvian garment
OTHER USES	a. In gold or silver kid applied to a lined satin belt
	b. As a circular cap, with darts between each fish

Hemmed appliqué is a method that calls for simple shapes and thin material. The slub silk, uncomfortably thick, makes corners bulky and hard to turn. It was chosen because the color of the wrong side of the material could be used for the fishes. In hemmed appliqué a thin washable interlining helps to keep a shape accurately. Hemming should be invisible.

Although the fish cushion has been worked as a border both the fish and frog motifs can be used in a circle. If each motif touches the next one an attractive shape is formed in the center.

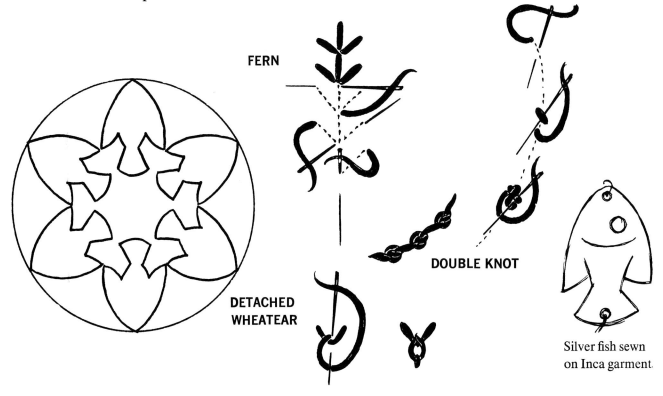

FERN

DOUBLE KNOT

DETACHED WHEATEAR

Silver fish sewn on Inca garment

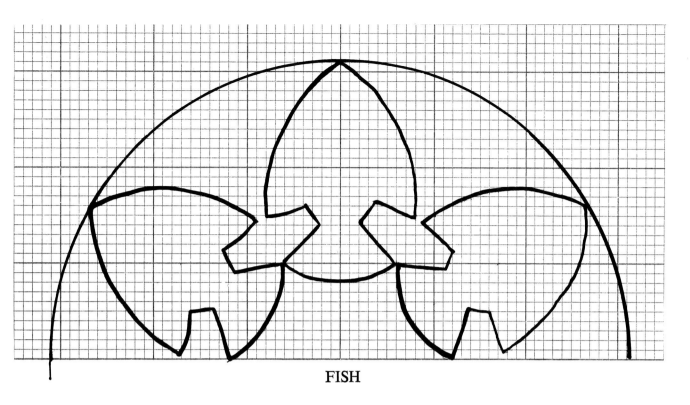

FISH

See page 1 for key to stitches.

Eye —
cut a hole in felt
to show background,
then work a star
in the space.

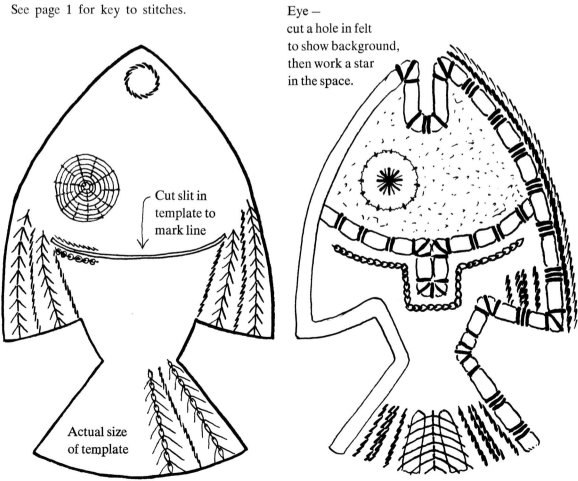

Cut slit in
template to
mark line

Actual size
of template

18

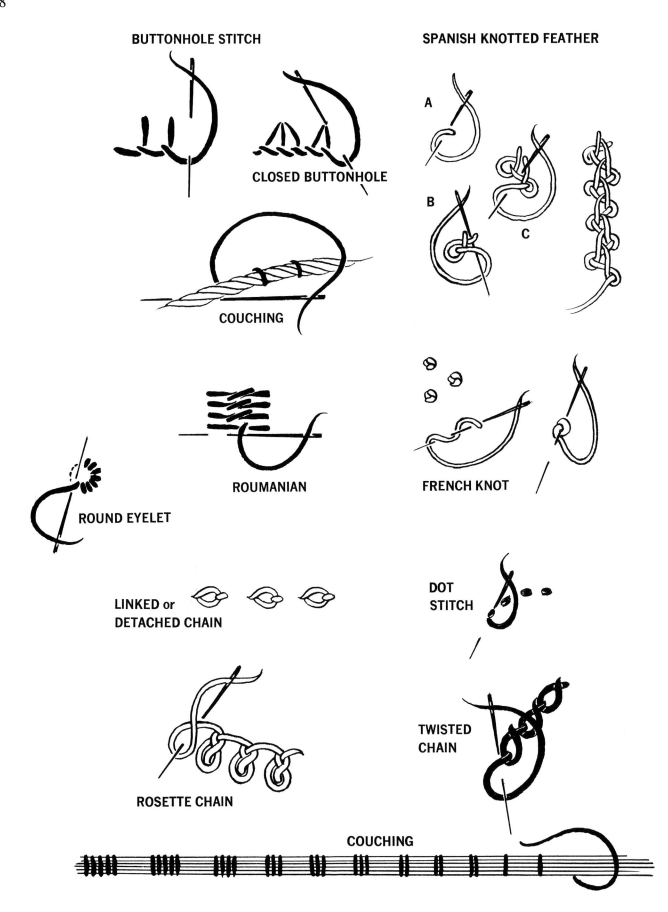

BUTTONHOLE STITCH

CLOSED BUTTONHOLE

SPANISH KNOTTED FEATHER

A

B

C

COUCHING

ROUMANIAN

ROUND EYELET

FRENCH KNOT

LINKED or
DETACHED CHAIN

DOT
STITCH

ROSETTE CHAIN

TWISTED
CHAIN

COUCHING

CUSHION/Bird

SEE PLATE 3.

FABRIC	Yellow linen
THREAD	White stranded cotton
STITCHES	Couching, double knot, stem, buttonhole wheel
SOURCE OF DESIGN	Pottery vessel, Highland Inca

Different arrangements of the simplified design immediately suggest other uses: large-scale curtaining and as accents on clothing and accessories.

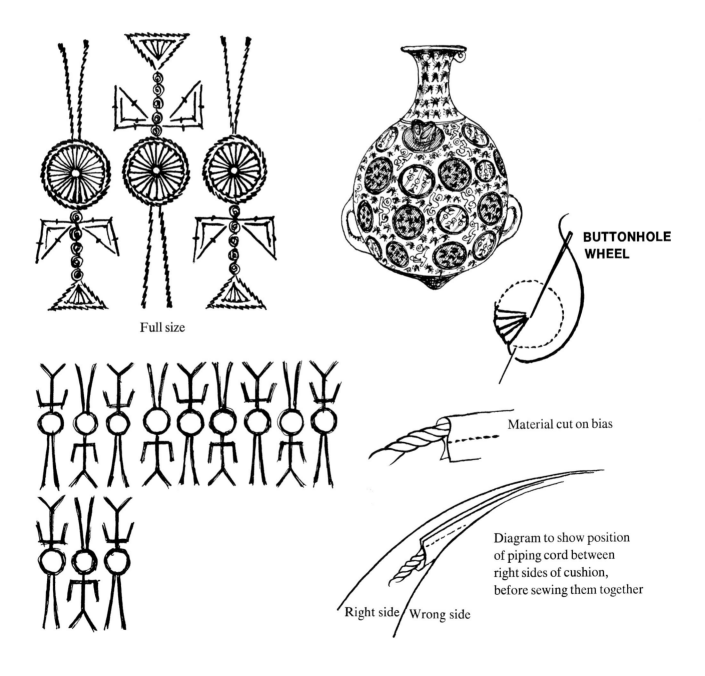

Full size

BUTTONHOLE WHEEL

Material cut on bias

Diagram to show position of piping cord between right sides of cushion, before sewing them together

Right side / Wrong side

CUSHION/Stylized Owl

FABRIC	Any firmly woven, richly colored material
THREAD	Crewel wool
COLOR	Choose deep rich colors such as royal blue, dark purple, plum, and dark turquoise; contrast these with soft dull yellows and lime green. A little salmon pink can be used as an accent.
STITCHES	The drawing shows several ways of combining a variety of stitches.
SOURCE OF DESIGN	A pottery warrior, Recuay
OTHER USES	a. Motif on a child's dress b. Cushion, as shown or circular using one of the owl's eyes.
HOW TO MAKE	Make up the cushion by machining the two sides together, right sides facing; leave a space in the long side for stuffing; turn to the right side, stuff and over sew the edges.

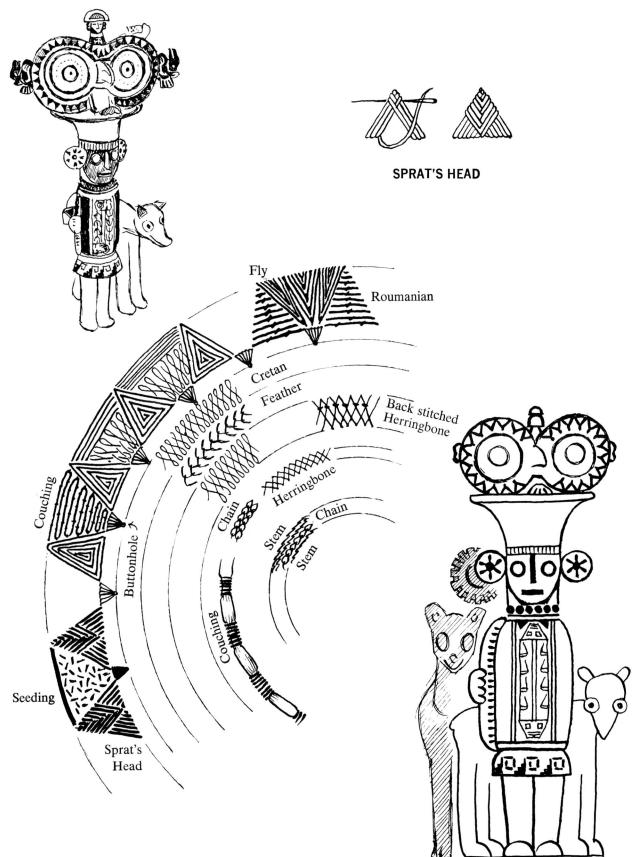

SPRAT'S HEAD

Fly

Roumanian

Cretan

Feather

Back stitched
Herringbone

Couching

Herringbone

Chain

Chain

Buttonhole

Stem

Stem

Couching

Seeding

Sprat's
Head

CUSHION or SOFT TOY/Fish

SEE PLATE 16.

FABRIC	Plain and patterned cotton
THREAD	Coton à broder
COLOR	Black and white
STITCHES	Closed buttonhole, double knot, star, stem
SOURCE OF DESIGN	A Mexican black-ware pottery bowl, partly unpolished
HOW TO MAKE	Quilt the fins. Apply the eye with a little padding beneath it; apply the mouth and plain material at the tail end. Place the right sides of body together and set the fins between them ready for machining. Turn the right way out ready for stuffing. Lightly pad the tail and quilt by machine. Stuff the body and sew it up. Embroider eye, stars near tail and other lines indicated.

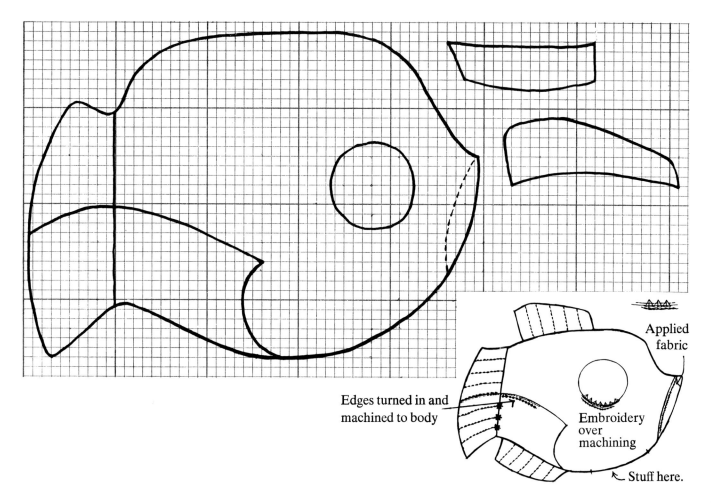

Applied fabric

Edges turned in and machined to body

Embroidery over machining

Stuff here.

CUSHION/Snake Design   SEE PLATE 11.

FABRIC	Single-thread canvas, 14 threads to the inch
THREAD	Tapestry wool, crewel, 3-ply wool
COLOR	*Backgrounds:* soft, deep pink, a blend of 3-ply wool and crewel wool, worked in Gobelin, trimmed with pink 3-ply wool *Snakes:* outlines in shades of gray wool, worked in satin stitch; eyes, turquoise wool *House:* outlined in gray and filled with paler turquoise and green of the same tone, worked in Gobelin
STITCHES	Straight Gobelin, satin
SOURCE OF DESIGN	A Nazca tapestry in which the background is rose-pink and the snakes are outlined with gray shell beads. The bodies of the snakes are filled in with blue and the house is filled in with tones of yellow. The work is irregular but evidently intended to be symmetrical.
OTHER USE	Stool top

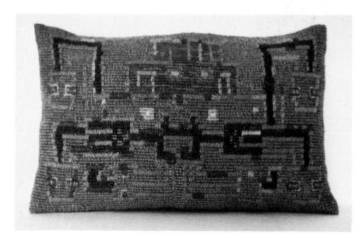

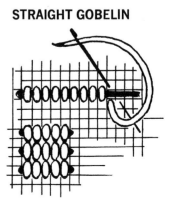

STRAIGHT GOBELIN

The symbols on the cartoon represent color change, not stitches.

SNAKE CUSHION

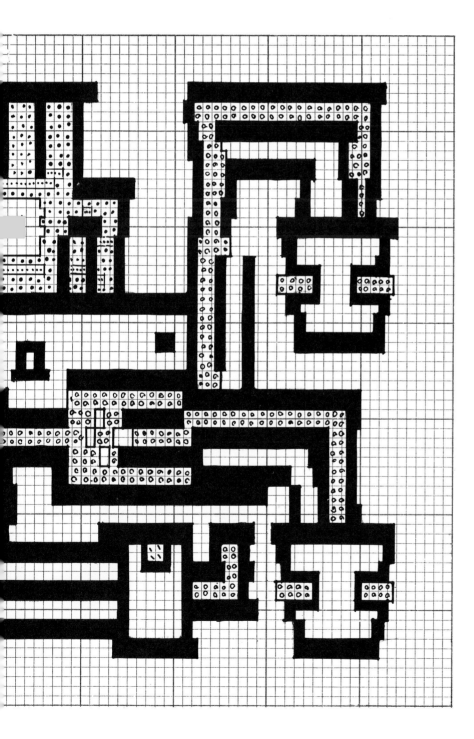

CUSHION / Warriors

SEE PLATE 10.

FABRIC	Single-thread canvas, 14 threads to the inch
THREAD	Tapestry wool, crewel, 3-ply wool
COLOR	*Faces:* grey; features, navy; eyes, pink tufts *Arms:* navy and purple with yellow tufts set in pink tent stitch *Body:* grey with navy and yellow pattern and purple tufts *Background:* soft dull turquoise
STITCHES	Cross, long-armed cross, diagonal Florentine, straight Gobelin, tent, tufting
SOURCE OF DESIGN	From a fragment of a garment woven to resemble tapestry, Tiahuanaco, Bolivia

The background is worked entirely in straight Gobelin stitch.

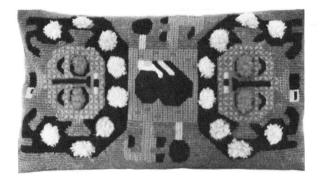

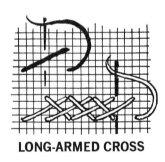

LONG-ARMED CROSS

REVERSE TENT

DIAGONAL FLORENTINE

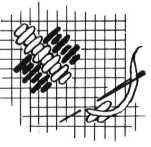

TENT

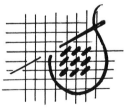

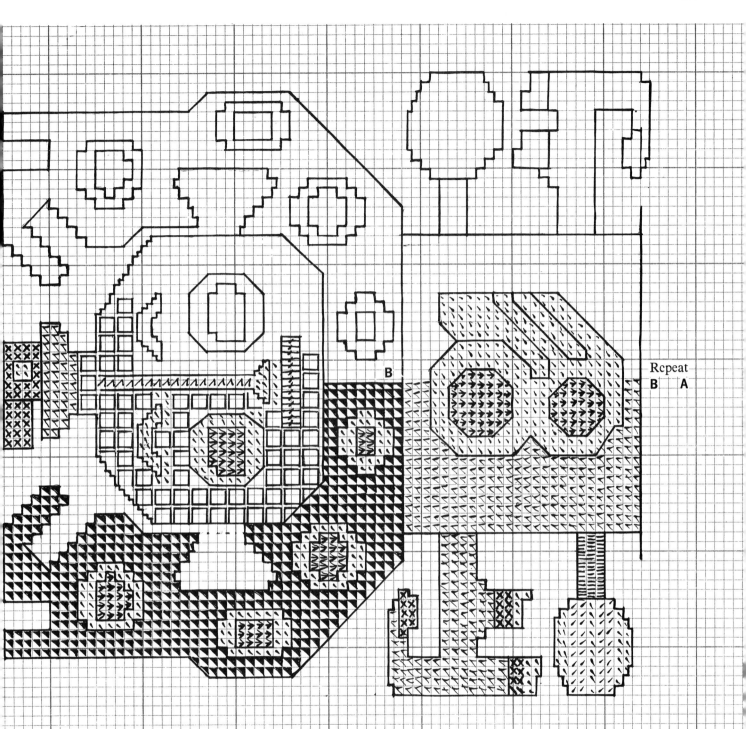

B

Repeat
B A

Symbol	Name	Symbol	Name	Symbol	Name
◣	Diagonal Florentine	✕	Cross	▢	Scottish
⋁	Tufting	⋀⋀⋀	Long-armed Cross	‖‖‖	Gobelin
╱	Tent	╪	Roumanian		

SCOTTISH

PATCHWORK FLOOR CUSHION

FABRIC	Strong cotton and denim
THREAD	Machine thread
COLOR	Shades of grey, purple, gold, turquoise, black, white
STITCHES	Web, Parisian, mosaic, cross, rice, small chequer, ray, long-armed cross, double cross, Gobelin or Florentine, flat
SOURCE OF DESIGN	A mirror-back, decorated with turquoise, shell, and colored stone mosaics, Tiahuanaco, Bolivia
OTHER USES	The design of four snakes and a human face could be used for canvas work as a cushion, stool top, or seat cover. The diagram below indicates the tone of the original and opposite some stitches are suggested. Their final choice depends on the size of the work.

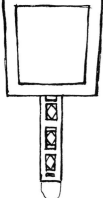

WEB STITCH

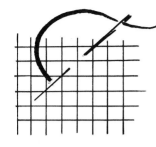

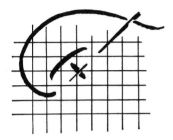

CUSHION or FLAT STITCH

Top

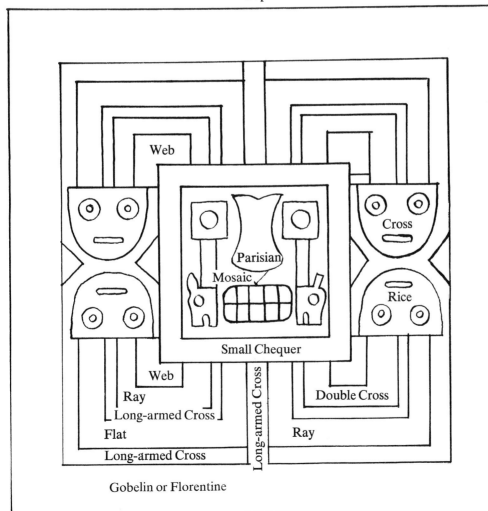

Web

Cross

Parisian

Mosaic

Rice

Small Chequer

Web

Ray

Long-armed Cross

Double Cross

Flat

Long-armed Cross

Ray

Long-armed Cross

Gobelin or Florentine

MOSAIC

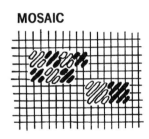

RAY

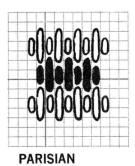

PARISIAN

TUFTED CUSHION

FABRIC	Burlap
THREAD	Various wools
COLOR	The feathers woven into the Peruvian work are brilliant shades of gold, orange, turquoise, and a rich, gleaming black
STITCHES	Tufting
SOURCE OF DESIGN	Feather hat, Tiahuanaco, Bolivia
HOW TO MAKE	Place right sides together; machine seams, taking care not to catch in any tufts.

Each color is a blend of either three different thicknesses of wool or three different shades and thicknesses. As with rug making, it is easier to work upward from the bottom row, always in the same direction. Keep the loops as nearly as possible the same length; cut when the work is finished. Natural variation in length improves the final result, which would lose some of its richness if the slightly uneven surface were sheared flat.

Burlap is a satisfactory foundation material; tufted rows will be 3 to 5 threads apart, according to the coarseness of the burlap and the weight of the wool.

In tufted work some areas can be left clear to incorporate the fabric color into the design, or part can be covered with long-armed cross-stitch.

SEE PLATE 5.

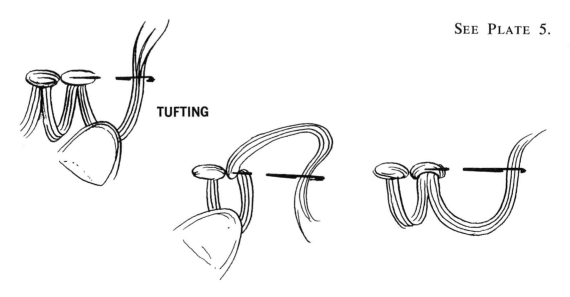

TUFTING

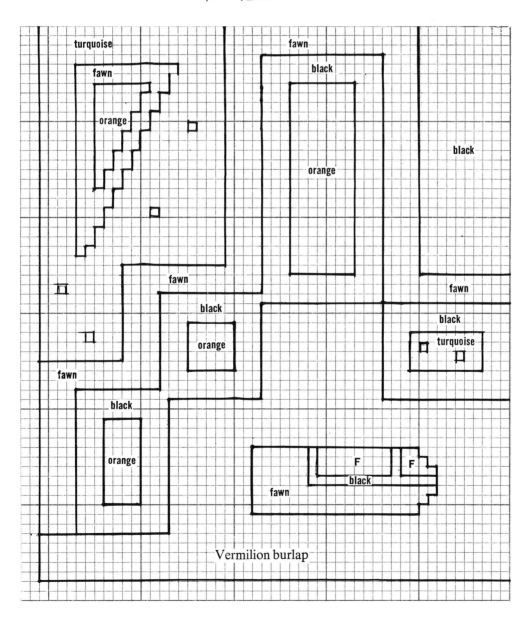

turquoise

fawn

black

fawn

orange

orange

black

fawn

fawn

black

fawn

black

orange

black

turquoise

fawn

black

orange

F   F

black

fawn

Vermilion burlap

CUSHION/Heads

FABRIC   Burlap or any loose, even weave

THREAD   Crewel and double knitting wool

COLOR
a. Orange, brown, ochre, cream, pink, turquoise
b. Soft royal blue, a little pale blue, various shades of dull yellow, brown, rusty pink, dull pea green, white
c. Dark brown, pale and golden yellow, royal blue, pink plum, shades of turquoise
d. Fawn, cream, chocolate, pink, white, with blue accents

STITCHES   Various surface stitches with small areas of tufting

SOURCE OF DESIGN   Paracas textiles

HOW TO MAKE   Make a set of cushions, each with a head which either fills the space or leaves a wide border. Vary the arrangement of tones so that the set of cushions is united by color. Work in a style similar to the lamp base (page 13) using a variety of surface stitches. Build up solid areas with closely packed rows or spread them out to vary the density of the filling. Crewel wool and double knitting change the size of the finished stitch; small areas of tufting give further contrast.

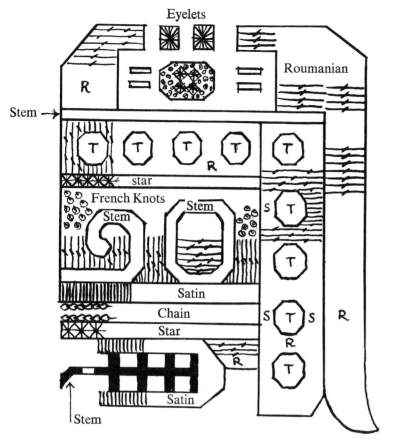

Eyelets

Roumanian

Stem →

R

star

French Knots

Stem   Stem

Satin

Chain

Star

Satin

Stem

R = Roumanian

T = Tufting

S = Satin

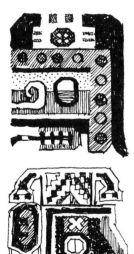

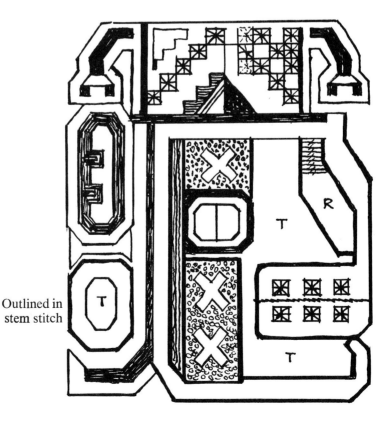

Outlined in
stem stitch

CUSHION/Diamond Pattern SEE PLATE 16.

FABRIC	Red even-weave cotton
THREAD	Coton à broder
COLOR	White cotton; a line of black can be introduced
STITCHES	Bosnian, cross
SOURCE OF DESIGN	Knotted textile, a headdress 1⅞ inches wide

Possible repeat positions are shown below.

A. End to end
B. Sideways
C. Interlocking diamonds
D. As worked on the cushion in the photograph. See color plate 16.

A

Border

BOSNIAN

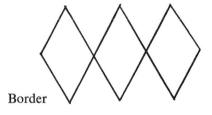

B Border

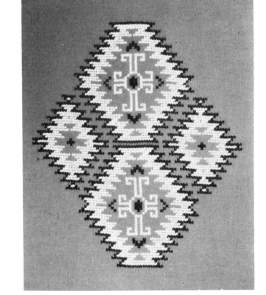

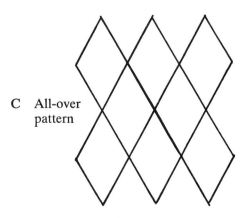

C All-over pattern

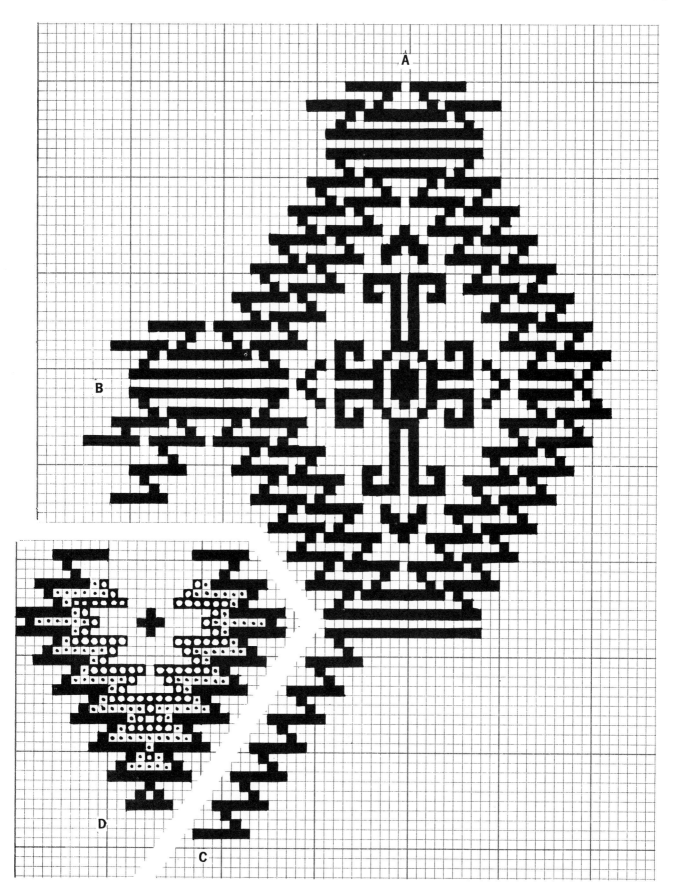

CUSHION/Geometric Design

FABRIC	Canvas
THREAD	Crewel or tapestry wool
COLOR	Several shades of two contrasting colors
STITCHES	Byzantine, fishbone, Hungarian point, mosaic, irregular satin, cross, double cross, Norwich, wheatsheaf, couching
SOURCE OF DESIGN	Suggested by an allover pattern on a poncho-shirt from the Inca period, Ica Valley, Peru

Diagrams shows four ways to turn a corner. Four ways of filling a square, two treatments of the diagonal line, and several ways of arranging the repeat.

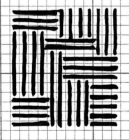

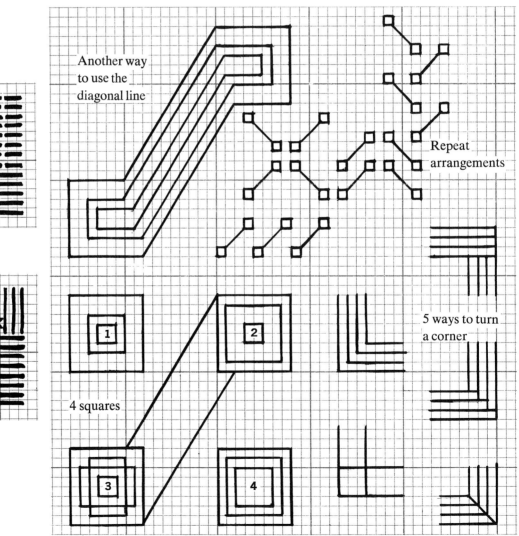

Another way to use the diagonal line

Repeat arrangements

5 ways to turn a corner

4 squares

1 2 3 4

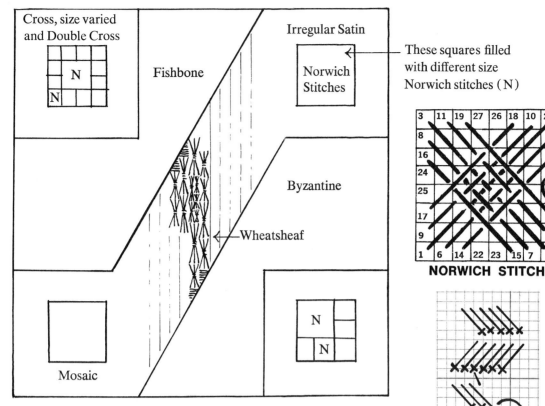

NORWICH STITCH

FISHBONE

Suggested stitch arrangement for each square. Flop design and work in contrasting colors.

An alternate selection of stitches.

The same basic design with a wider diagonal line worked in heavy couching

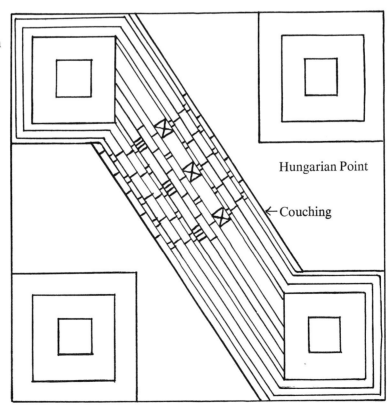

HOW TO MAKE UP
A CANVAS CUSHION

Prepare the canvas by turning back the edges close to the embroidery; tack firmly all round. Tack the linen and canvas together, leaving one end open for stuffing. Using thread to match the linen, oversew the materials together, stitching between each thread of the canvas so that the straight oversewing stitch slips down between the wool stitches and is hidden.

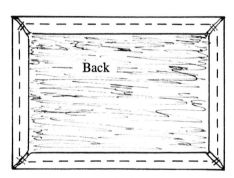

Back

Canvas turned to back
of work and tucked down

Front of embroidery

← Lining

Cotton pulled tightly out of sight

Represents
final line of embroidery

CUSHION/Geometric Design SEE PLATE 13.

FABRIC	Off-white coarsely woven cotton, uneven in texture but smoother than burlap
THREAD	Crewel, 3-ply knitting wool
COLOR	Navy blue, royal blue, 3 shades purple, 2 shades salmon pink, deep yellow, orange
STITCHES	Chain, rosette chain, twisted chain, detached chain, closed buttonhole, closed herringbone, couched fillings, dot, double knot, fly, long-armed feather
SOURCE OF DESIGN	Suggested by a Peruvian textile, Cooper-Hewitt Museum of Design, New York City
OTHER USES	a. Each motif can be used separately or a whole cushion can be worked using one repeat many times.
	b. A quilt, embroidered in wool on a plain blanket
HOW TO MAKE	When the embroidered side of the cushion is worked, cut the back material the same size, place right sides together, machine the seams, leaving a stuffing opening. Turn to the right side. Sew a cord to.match that used in the design along the seams. Side of each square about 4 inches.

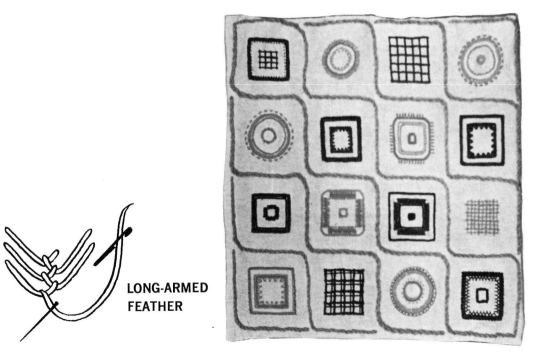

LONG-ARMED
FEATHER

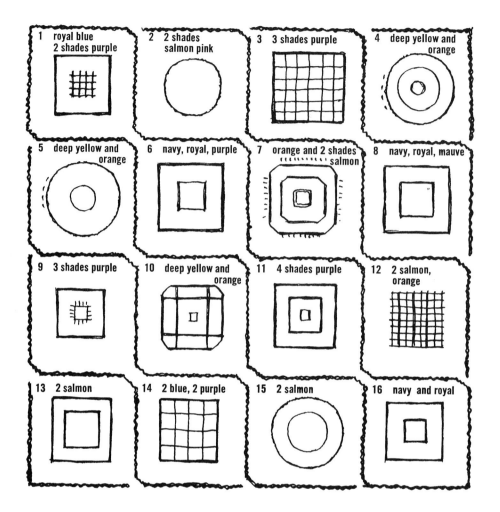

1 royal blue 2 shades purple	2 2 shades salmon pink	3 3 shades purple	4 deep yellow and orange
5 deep yellow and orange	6 navy, royal, purple	7 orange and 2 shades salmon	8 navy, royal, mauve
9 3 shades purple	10 deep yellow and orange	11 4 shades purple	12 2 salmon, orange
13 2 salmon	14 2 blue, 2 purple	15 2 salmon	16 navy and royal

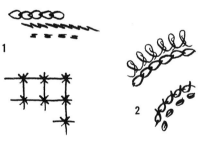

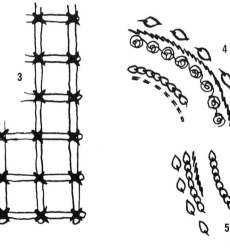

See page 1 for key to stitches.

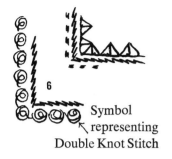

6 Symbol representing Double Knot Stitch

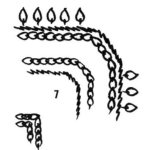

7

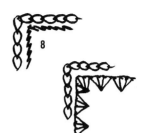

8

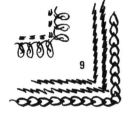

9

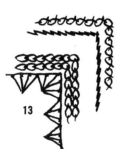

10 Long-armed Feather

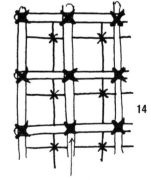

11 Closed Herringbone

12

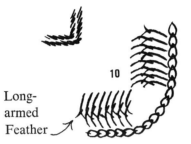

13

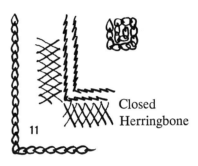

14 Couched Fillings

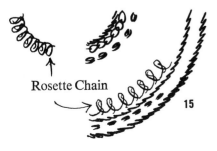

Rosette Chain

15

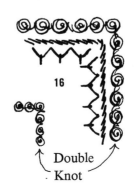

16 Double Knot

WASTE PAPER BASKET I SEE PLATE 8.

FABRIC	Orange red slub silk upholstery fabric
THREAD	Crewel wool, stranded cotton
COLOR	Several shades of orange red, vermilion and very dark red, shades of soft turquoise, gray, gray blue, stone, pea green, yellow, and pink
STITCHES	Stem, Cretan, buttonhole wheel
SOURCE OF DESIGN	Chimu painted cotton textile, brown on a white ground. In the original design each panel is slightly narrower than shown. The correct proportion would have made too narrow a cylinder to be practical for a wastepaper basket
OTHER USES	Each square can decorate a bag, cuchion or pocket

The photographs show the design before and after it was made up to the original arrangement. A space was left between strips so that they could be separated. After each side seam was sewn, the lower band was tacked into place and hemmed to the top band. The embroidery was fitted over a strong cardboard drum and finished with Contact lining.

Position while working

Rearrangement when made up

Pattern
on bottom row

CRETAN

See page 1 for key to stitches.

OTHER MOTIFS USED
ON WASTE PAPER BASKET

WASTEPAPER BASKET II SEE PLATE 10.

FABRIC   White burlap

THREAD   Rug, crewel and 3 ply wool, pearl cotton

COLOR   Chocolate brown, 3 shades rust, golden yellow, cream

STITCHES   Closed herringbone, couching, eyelets

SOURCE OF DESIGN   A tripod vessel from the State of Oaxaca, Mexico. The pottery is painted in deep, rich colors ranging from orange to reddish brown on a biscuit ground

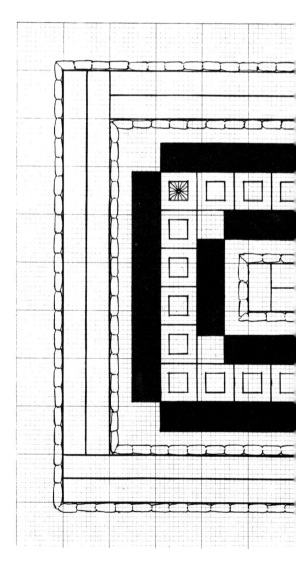

OTHER USES   a. Long cushion or bolster
                            b. Bag
                            c. Curtain hem

HOW TO MAKE   For waste paper basket, see page 42.

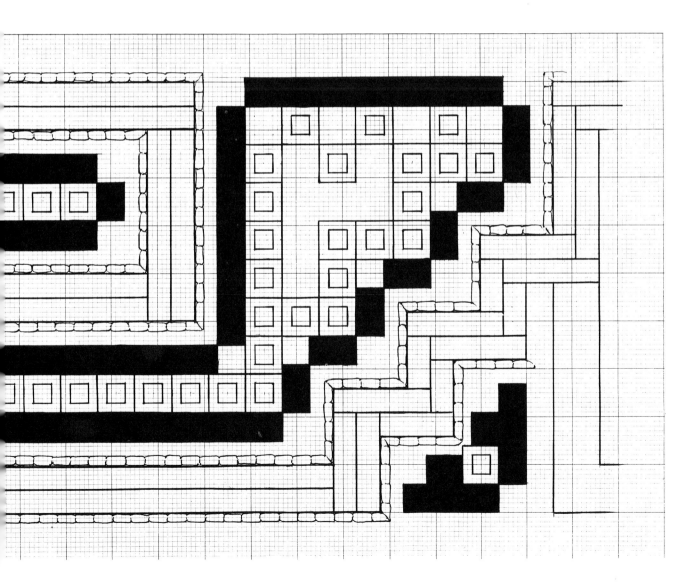

CANVAS WORK EXAMPLES

Diagrams A and B are the same pattern arranged differently on the canvas. C and D show changes that can be made by altering the tone of the stripes. Test this out on paper before working.

FABRIC	Single-thread canvas, 14 threads to inch, for all examples
A. B. C. D. THREAD	Tapestry wool
COLOR	3 shades of one color and 2 other colors
STITCHES	A. Satin, tent, star. B. C. D. Star, diagonal, Florentine

A.

SOURCE OF DESIGN   Paracas style spouted pottery painted in red, yellow, black, and white

USES   Upholstery, bags, purses

This pattern is not restricted to Pre-Columbian art and its similarity to basket weaving is obvious. Although it looks simple to work, it is quite easy for one to get lost. The Peruvian potter either became muddled or found that the two ends of the pattern did not join together as he hoped.

B.

C.

D.

SEE PLATE 4.

CANVAS WORK EXAMPLES

E. F.	THREAD	Tapestry wool, 3-ply wool, stranded cotton
	COLOR	Several shades of 2 or 3 colors, according to choice, or see color plate 15.
	STITCHES	Cross, double cross, long-armed cross, straight Gobelin, Satin, straight, tent, back, Hungarian
SOURCE OF DESIGN		Bolivian pottery

E.

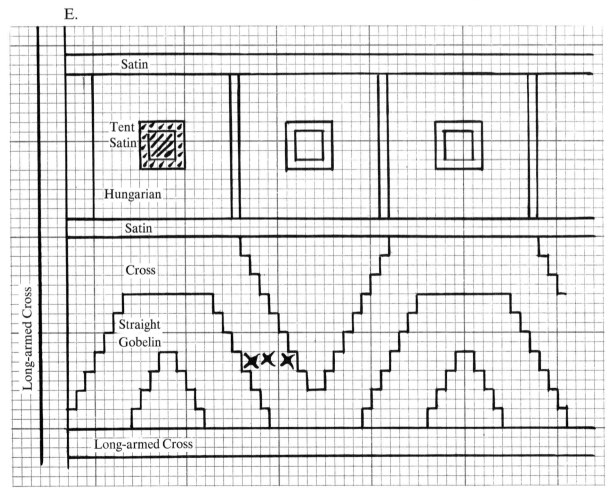

Although these two patterns hold together well on the original painted pottery, they do not combine successfully on canvas. For this reason the diagrams are separated.

F.

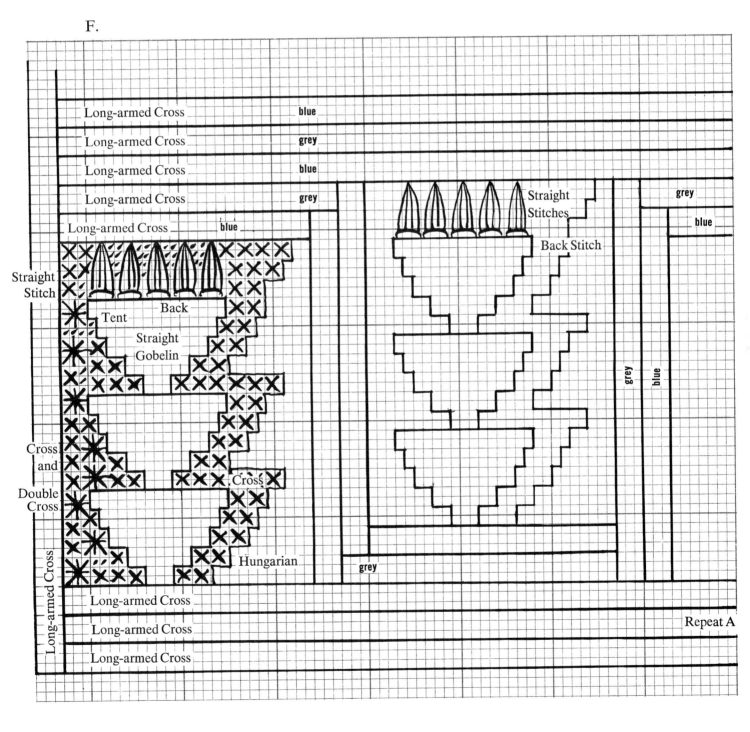

CANVAS WORK EXAMPLES

G. THREAD, COLOR
AND STITCHES

Background: diagonal Florentine stitch in rust red homespun wool, over worked with an occasional stitch of vermilion stranded cotton

Outline: cross stitch, fawn 3 ply wool

Hungarian filling: alternate rows black and dark brown 3 ply wool

Chequer stitch: yellow crewel wool

Tent stitch: black crewel

Wheatsheaf: needle threaded with 2 shades turquoise crewel

SOURCE OF DESIGN

Vessel in human shape—Paracas, Cavernas, Peru

SEE PLATE 5.

G.

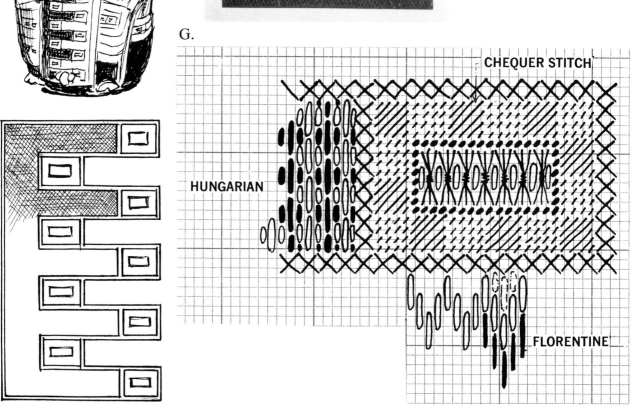

CHEQUER STITCH

HUNGARIAN

FLORENTINE

H.	THREAD	Tapestry wool
	COLOR	Interlocking spirits royal blue and pale turquoise; bird, dark turquoise against pale lime green; eye, navy and red; beak and body spots, lemon yellow
	STITCHES	Florentine stitch. This design could also be worked in cross-stitch, counted satin, or in large-scale darning on filigree net curtaining. The cartoon shows how the design connects and repeats. The spirals interlock.
SOURCE OF DESIGN		A typical Peruvian bird design from a poncho

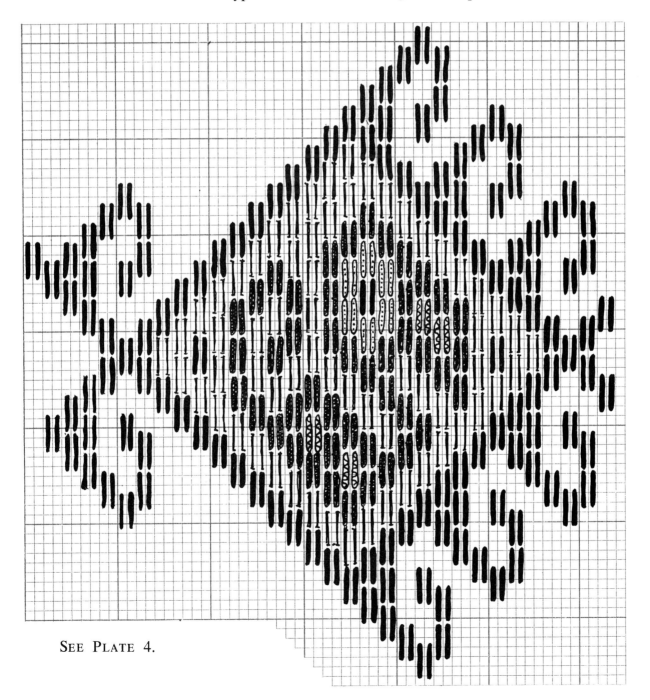

SEE PLATE 4.

CANVAS WORK EXAMPLES

I. CONTINUOUS SNAKES

Peruvian textile workers created many ingenious patterns with fish, birds and reptiles. Many are difficult to copy and extremely tantalizing because they look so much simpler than in fact they are. One small mistake can throw the whole design out of gear.

These snakes can be used as a border either vertically or horizontally, or as an all-over pattern. The whole design should be drawn on graph paper before embroidery is commenced. If this appears to be a tedious exercise it is far better to discover how the design works on paper than to have to unpick mistakes on fabric.

Suitable for cross stitch on even weave material.

Use one color.

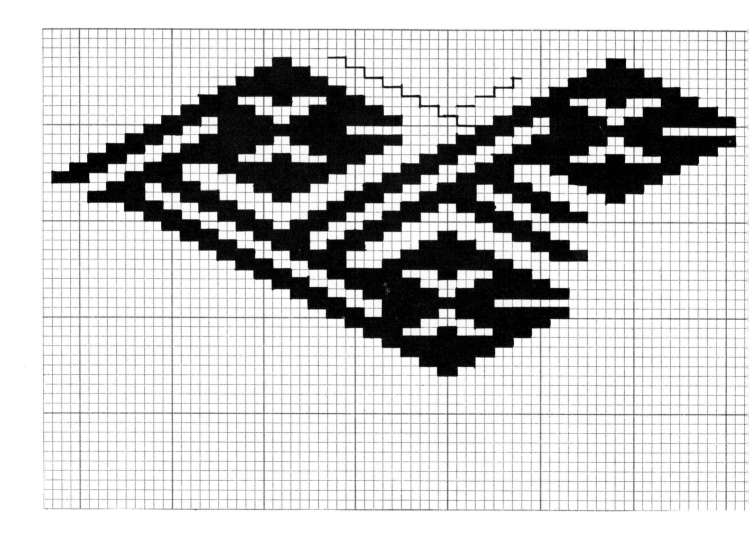

J. SNAKE DESIGN

Suitable for an all-over pattern on canvas or even-weave linen. If on canvas, work the snakes in rows alternately dark and light, and the spaces between in a different color and mid-tone.

If worked on even-weave material, do not embroider over the spaces because the appearance of the fabric is pleasant to look at.

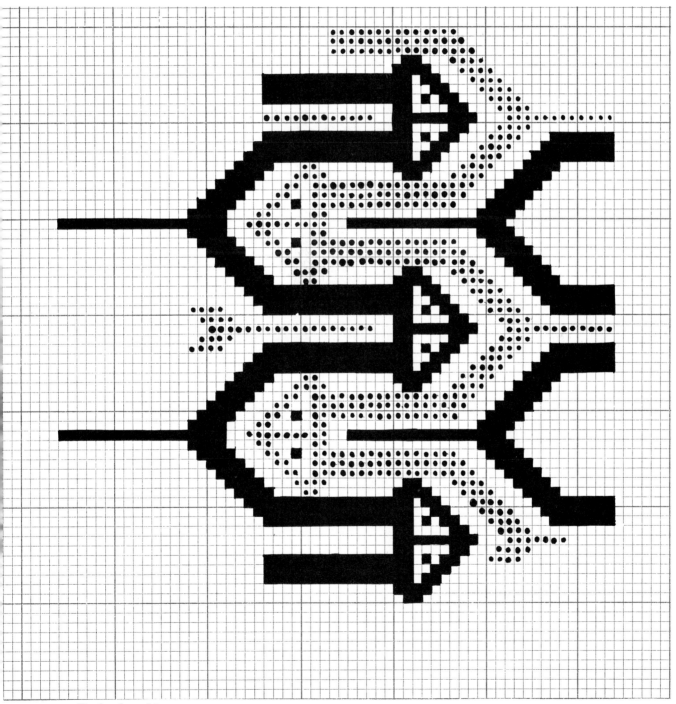

Design from Nazca pottery

DOORSTOP MADE WITH TWO WEIGHTS

SEE PLATE 12.

FABRIC	Burlap in green and 2 shades of grey
THREAD, COLOR	Crewel, tapestry, 3-ply knitting wool, in green, lime and chocolate
	Wool, green, lime, chocolate
	Pearl cotton No. 5, cream
STITCHES	Back, couching, fly, stem, Roumanian
SOURCE	Mixtec gold and turquoise jewel—Oaxaca, Mexico

Neither weight had a flat surface at top or bottom. Circles of card corrected this and made a better surface for sticking down the burlap.

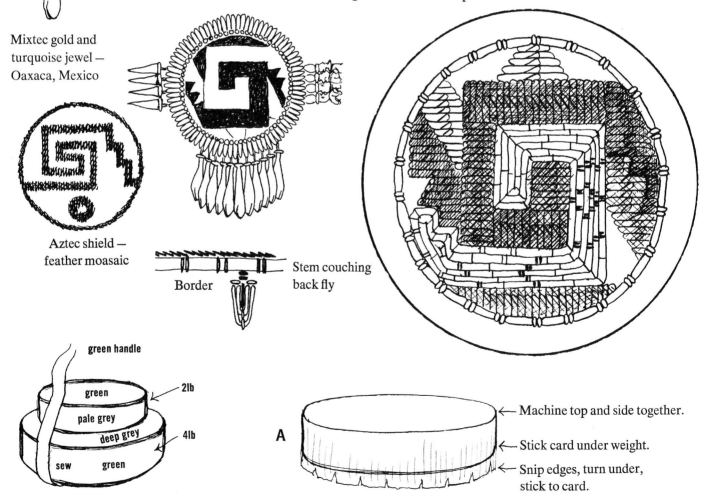

Mixtec gold and turquoise jewel — Oaxaca, Mexico

Aztec shield — feather moasaic

Border

Stem couching back fly

green handle

green
pale grey
deep grey
sew   green

2lb
4lb

A

← Machine top and side together.

← Stick card under weight.

← Snip edges, turn under, stick to card.

INTERLOCKING SPIRAL DESIGN

FABRIC	Cream homespun cotton
THREAD	Crewel wool
COLOR	Brown
STITCH	Counted satin
SOURCE OF DESIGN	Stone Mosaic, on a building at Mitla, Mexico
USE	Small purse, glasses case or as an all-over pattern

This apparently simple design is confusing to work. Embroider in one color only; the other is formed by the background spaces. Count threads carefully and test on spare fabric to discover the best size to work.

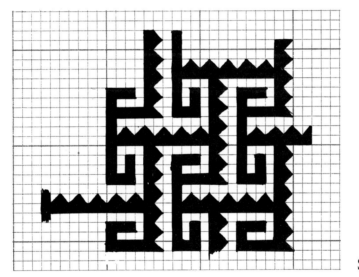

SEE PLATE 4.

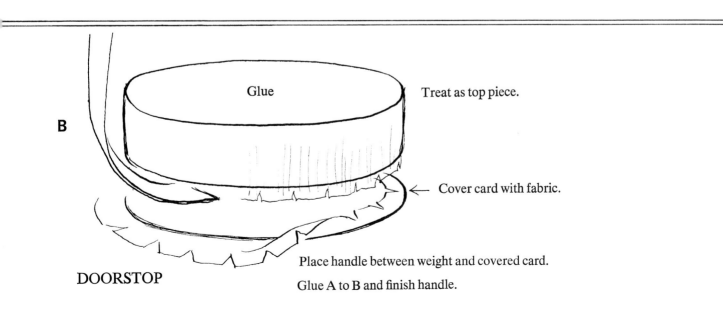

B

Glue

Treat as top piece.

← Cover card with fabric.

Place handle between weight and covered card.

DOORSTOP

Glue A to B and finish handle.

TABLECLOTH

FABRIC	Organdy
THREAD	Stranded cotton, one strand
COLOR	Dark and light brown, blue, grey, pale green, yellow, white
STITCHES	Back, buttonhole, chain, closed herringbone, eyelets, satin, stem, coral knot, fern, feather, and twisted chain can also be used
SOURCE	Mochica pottery, Peru

To transfer the design, place the sketch under the organdy and trace with a very hard pencil (2H), which should not soil the working thread. If in doubt, use an extremely fine painted line. Some stitches are worked on the back, others on the front. See page 60.

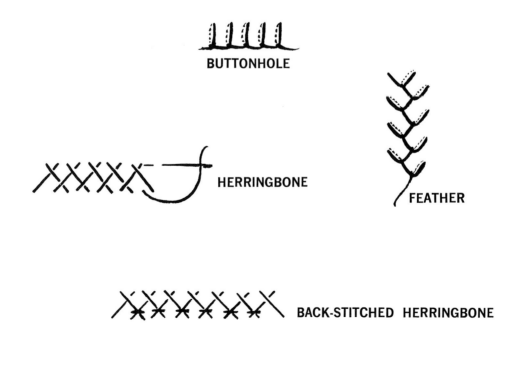

BUTTONHOLE

HERRINGBONE

FEATHER

BACK-STITCHED HERRINGBONE

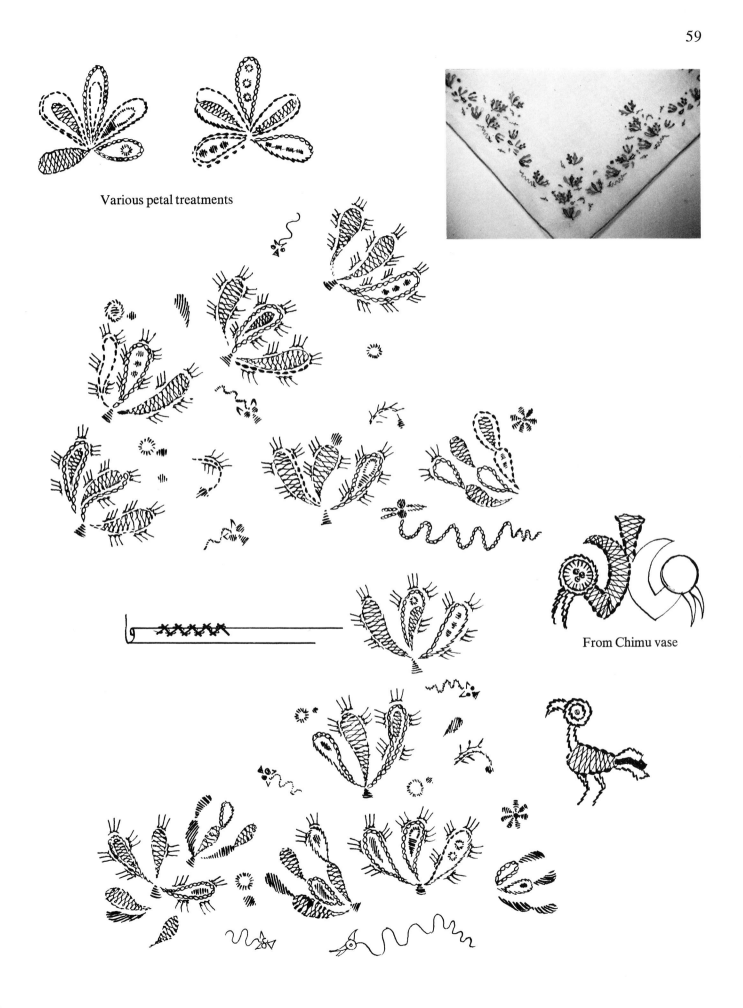

Various petal treatments

From Chimu vase

The beginning and ending of embroidery thread should always be hidden. On organdy this is particularly difficult because the material is fine and transparent. At the beginning leave a long enough end to thread in later, when enough stitchery is completed. The diagrams of closed herringbone show the wrong and right ways of dealing with the problem.

Organdy is rebellious material and edge neatening demands patience because it is difficult to scratch a line straight on the thread and generally impossible to draw a thread out. Cutting straight is also very hard to do. Edges must be straightened before embroidery is begun. The easiest method, other than binding, is to turn a small hem to the right side and to decorate it with threaded herringbone.

Ends are run in through the stitches picking up a tiny amount of material, just enough to prevent the thread from slipping into the center.

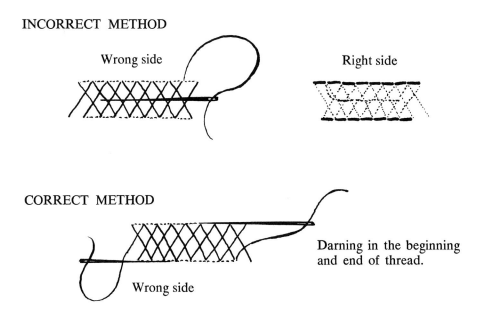

INCORRECT METHOD

Wrong side

Right side

CORRECT METHOD

Darning in the beginning and end of thread.

Wrong side

TRAY CLOTH I

FABRIC	Yellow even-weave
THREAD	Stranded cotton, deeper yellow than fabric
STITCHES	Back, cross, four-sided, star
SOURCE OF DESIGN	Pottery dish in the museum at Cuzco, Peru

Make matching napkins with the edges hemstitched and fringed. See page 67.

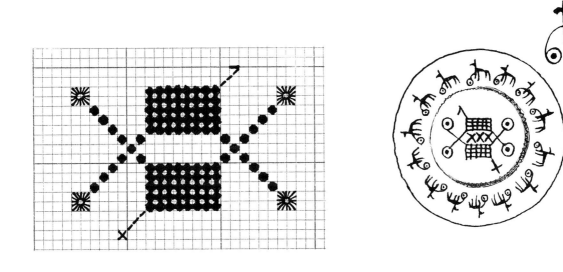

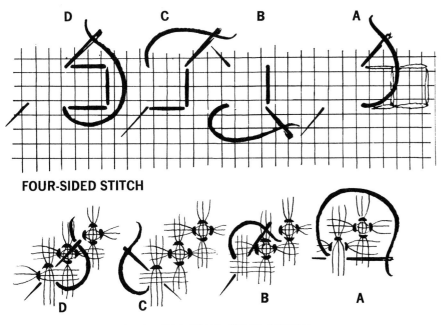

FOUR-SIDED STITCH

DIAGONAL METHOD FOR FOUR-SIDED STITCH

TRAY CLOTH II

SEE PLATE 2.

FABRIC	Organdy
THREAD	Stranded cotton
COLOR	White or deeper shade of whatever is chosen for organdy
STITCHES	Back, double back, spider web, stem, twisted chain
SOURCE OF DESIGN	Pottery, Lima
HOW TO MAKE	Bind the top edge of the pocket. Tack in place in the corner, and hem the free edge to the cloth. Bind each end, thus securing the other side of the pocket. Machine the binding and cloth, right sides together. Turn binding over and hem into back of machine stitches. Bind long sides in same way, carefully turning in the corners and over-sewing the ends.

Spots are useful alone, in rows or all-over patterns. They can be placed in the corner of napkins and along the edge of tray cloths. On cushions they will scatter in different sizes or arrange formally in rows, or make a chequer pattern.

On clothing they may be isolated on pockets or repeated alternately in different tones on belts and other dress accessories.

HOW TO BIND AN OUTSIDE EDGE

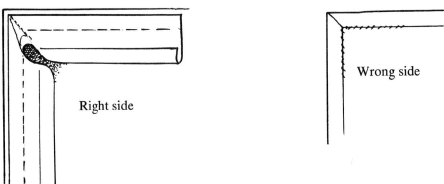

Right side

Wrong side

ORGANDY TRAYCLOTH

Ring of Twisted Chain
added to embroidery

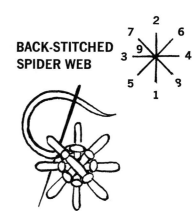

**BACK-STITCHED
SPIDER WEB**

Pottery motif — Lima

Take only one line
of stem stitch
to the centre
to avoid a tangle.

From pottery

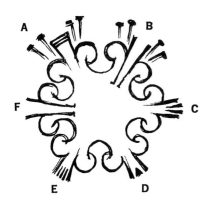

A   B

F   C

E   D

6 interpretations of
a simple motif, from pottery

Double Knot in thicker
thread

Chain

Stem

Star

Stem

Buttonhole
wheel

An occasional
square motif
helps to vary
a spot pattern.

STAR STITCH

Showing tie thread

Finish

TRAY CLOTH III

FABRIC	White cotton
THREAD	Coton à broder
COLOR	Blue
STITCHES	Chain, four-sided, eyelet, satin, stem
EDGES	Sides hemstitched; ends hemmed and covered with cotton fringe
SOURCE OF DESIGN	A highly stylized cat, which on some Paracas pots is more easily recognizable than on others. Diagram B is more obscure than Diagram A.
OTHER USE	On a pocket

A

Chain outline
4 sided
Eyelet
Stem

Derived from
incised motifs on
Paracas pottery bowl

B

Motifs on double spouted jar

Lower corner of cloth

Distance
from fringe

Distance from hem

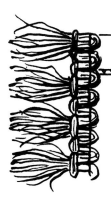

Traycloth-sides hemstitched:
ends covered with fringe

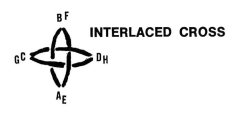

INTERLACED CROSS

All these designs are derived
from incised motifs on
Paracas pottery bowls

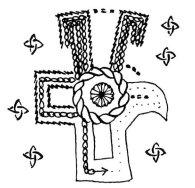

Motif suitable for traycloth or
decoration on a garment

HEMSTITCH METHOD

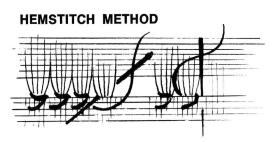

DESIGN MOTIF/Snake

SEE PLATE 9.

FABRIC	Open-weave linen
THREAD	Coton à broder
COLOR	White
STITCHES	Four-sided, satin, ringed back
SOURCE OF DESIGN	Gold repoussé work representing a puma skin with a three-dimensional head, Mochica (Peru). The tongue bears a human face and the body has a design of double-headed serpents. The puma's body is double, forming a pouch.
OTHER USES	a. Central border on a narrow runner b. Borders on a fine woolen stole c. Stripes on a curtain d. Allover stripes on a cushion e. Lampshade

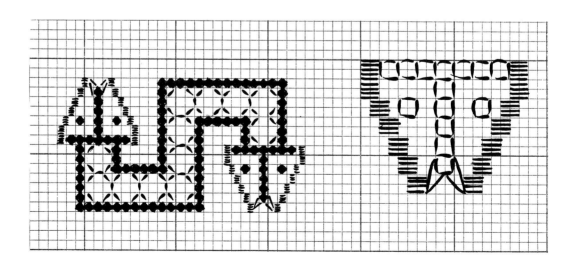

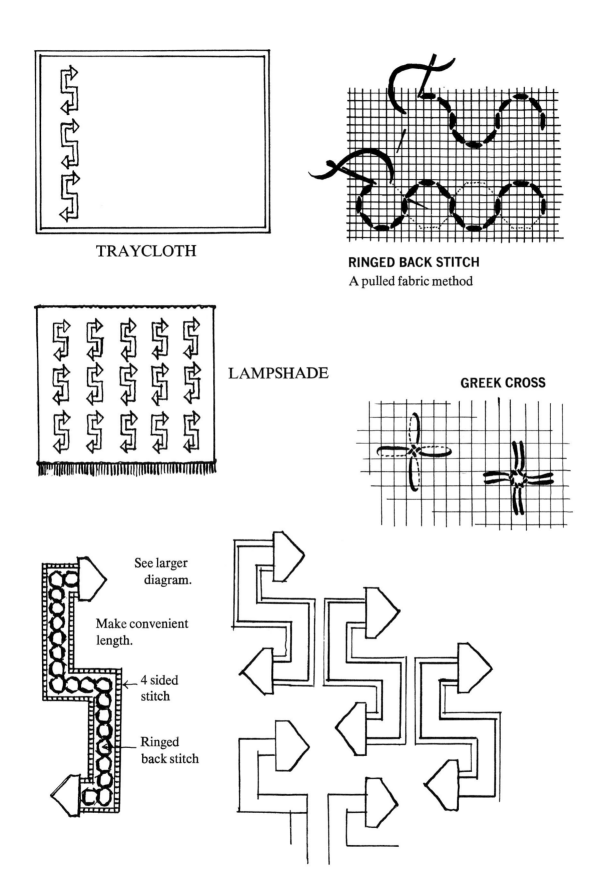

TRAYCLOTH

RINGED BACK STITCH
A pulled fabric method

LAMPSHADE

GREEK CROSS

See larger
diagram.

Make convenient
length.

4 sided
stitch

Ringed
back stitch

NAPKIN RINGS

SEE PLATE 7.

FABRIC	Coarse linen, double thread
THREAD	Pearl cotton No. 5
COLOR	White or cream, black
STITCHES	Counted satin, star
SOURCE OF DESIGN	Geometric pattern on pottery
USES	Border patterns

Although paper napkins have at the moment almost supplanted linen napkins, the fashion pendulum swings to and fro and these simple designs may instead find a use on place settings.

All the borders translate easily into canvas work and change with little trouble into allover patterns. They can be used for dress accessories or to accentuate a feature of a garment.

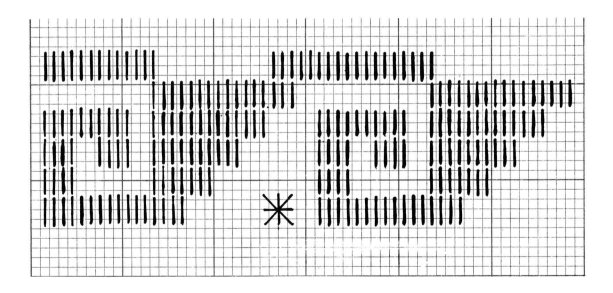

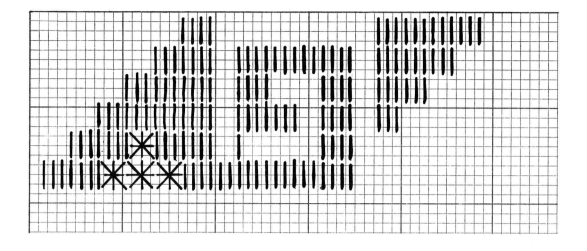

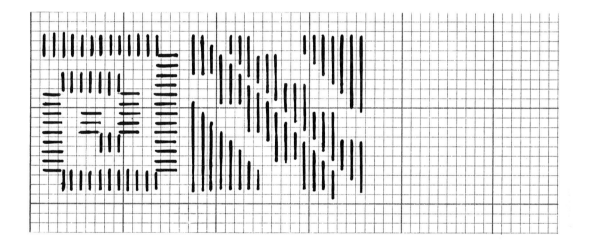

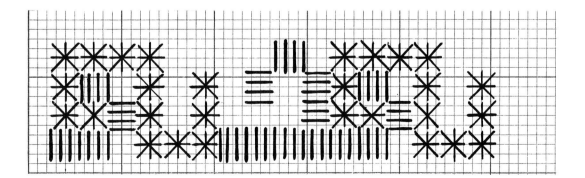

CURTAIN BORDER

SEE PLATE 6.

FABRIC	Needle run net
THREAD	Stranded cotton
STITCHES	Darning, closed herringbone, surface stitchery
SOURCE OF DESIGN	A clay urn, Amazon Delta
SUGGESTED USES	Curtains, sheer blouse.

DARNING ON NET

After the design is made it is traced on to glazed linen over which the net is firmly tacked and upon which it remains until work is complete.

Always work with a thick thread, preferably using all six strands of stranded cotton. Use a blunt needle (tapestry) for the actual running but use a fairly large crewel needle for darning the ends back into the stitcher so that they are completely hidden. It should never be possible to see beginnings and endings at a glance. This technical difficulty controls the design, making isolated stitches almost impossible.

A Darned net

B Shadow (closed herringbone) and surface stitchery

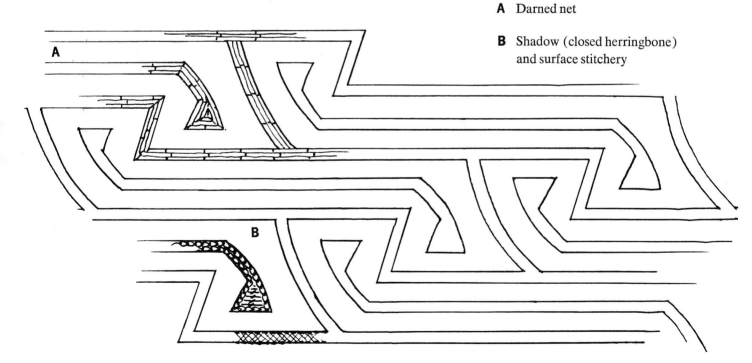

PLATE 1

See page 84.

PLATE 2

See pages 60, 61, 62, 64.

PLATE 3

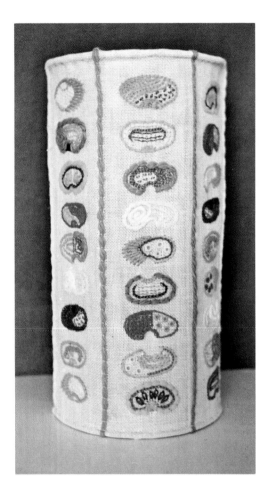

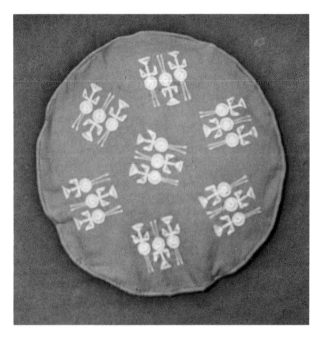

See pages 7, 19, 99, 101, 127.

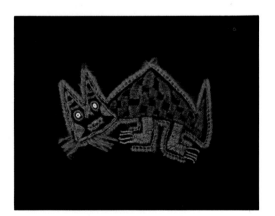

PLATE 4

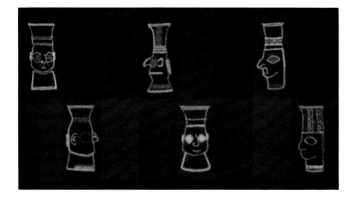

See pages 48, 53, 57, 96, 121, 124.

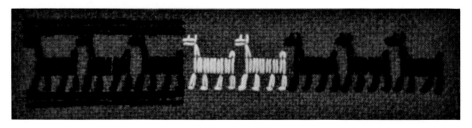

PLATE 5

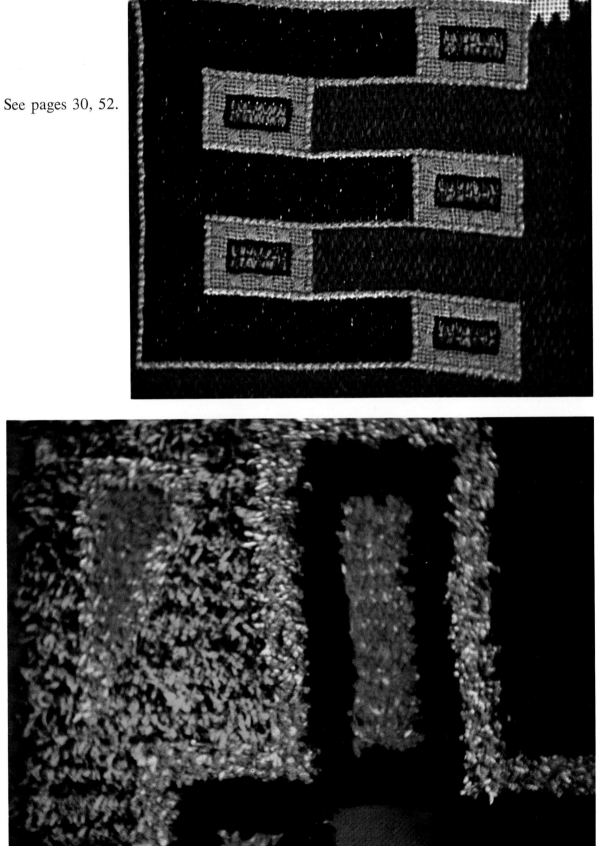

See pages 30, 52.

PLATE 6

See pages 70, 76, 116.

PLATE 7

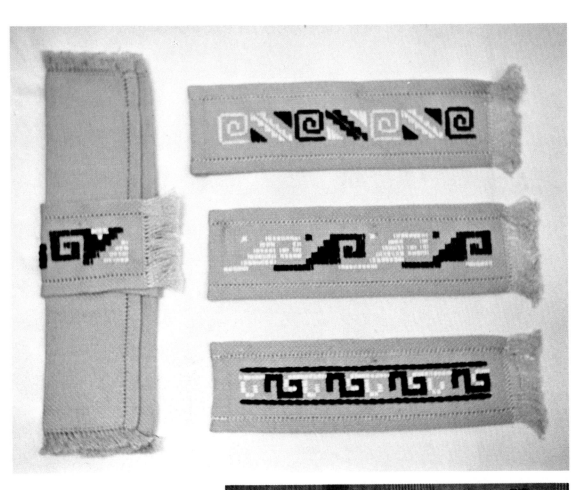

See pages 68, 76.

PLATE 8

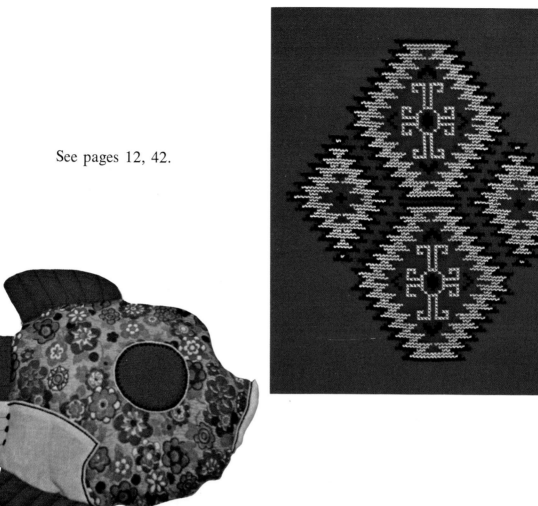

See pages 12, 42.

PLATE 9

See pages 66, 72, 78.

PLATE 10

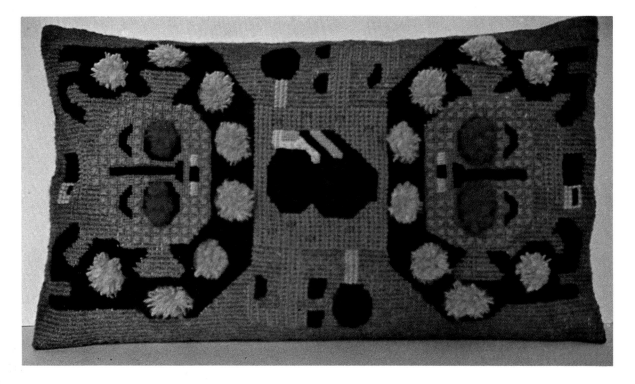

See pages 26, 46.

PLATE 11

See pages 23, 82.

PLATE 12

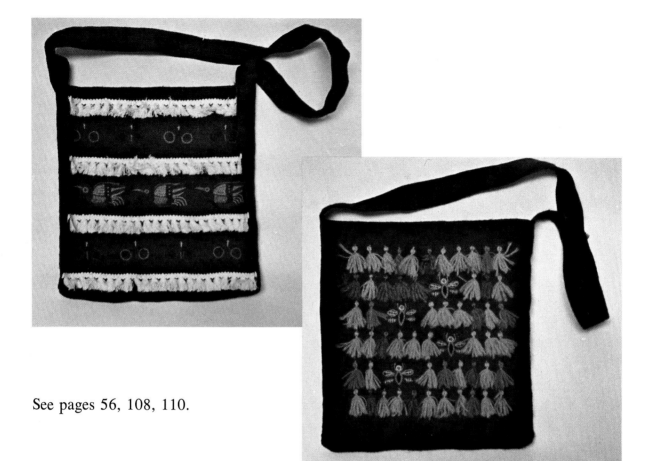

See pages 56, 108, 110.

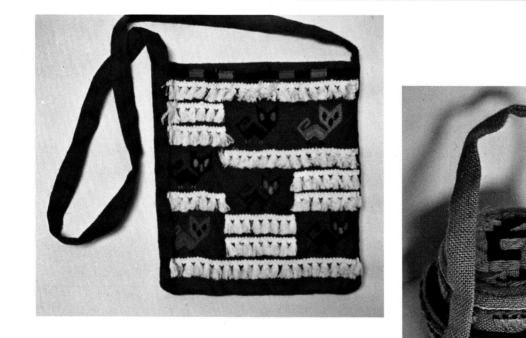

PLATE 13

See pages 39, 118.

PLATE 14

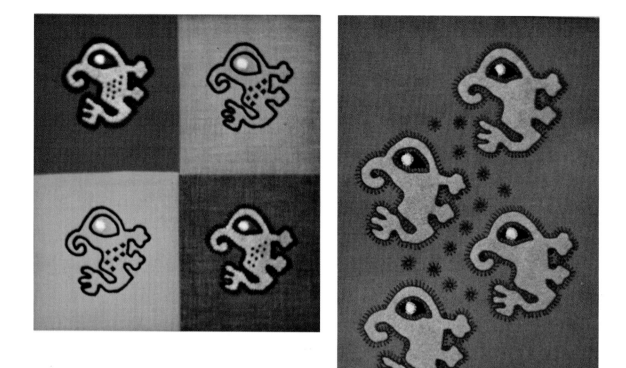

See pages 80, 98.

PLATE 15

See pages 50, 122.

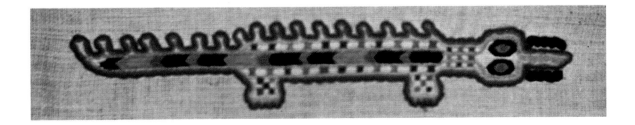

PLATE 16

See pages 22, 34, 102.

SQUARE NET CLOTH

FABRIC	Cream fine net
THREAD	Stranded cotton
COLOR	Chocolate and white
STITCHES	Darning, double running
SOURCE OF DESIGN	Pottery vessel, an aryballus, Cuzco region, Peru
SUGGESTED USES	a. Table cloth
	b. Larger type square scarf
	c. Sandwich plate cover

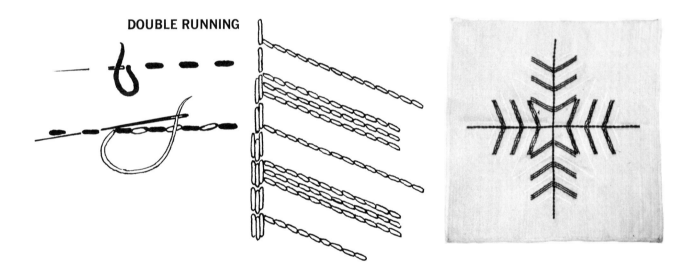

DOUBLE RUNNING

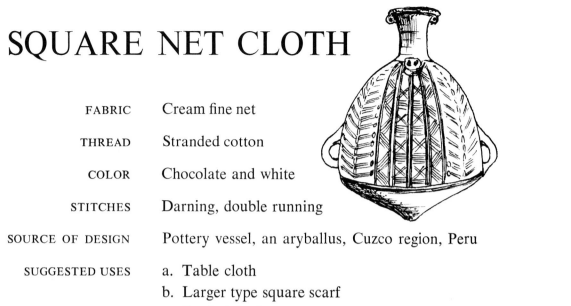

An interesting design made
by changing direction

MOTIF FOR USE ON OPEN-WEAVE LINEN — SEE PLATE 9.

FABRIC	Open-weave linen
THREAD	Stranded cotton
STITCHES	Counted satin, diagonal chained border, four-sided, Greek cross
SOURCE OF DESIGN	A Mayan Stone Mosaic on the Façade of the "Nunnery," Uxmal, Mexico
USES	a. Table linen on even-weave material
	b. Cushion on scrim with colored lining to show through

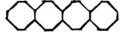
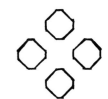
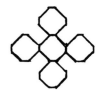
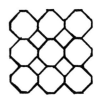

Various arrangements of motif

QUILT DESIGNS

A.   FABRIC   Good quality cotton

     THREAD   Coton à broder

     COLOR   Either different tones of the background or a variety of rich colors arranged so that adjacent squares are always different

     STITCHES   Rows of stem or chain, the number depending on the size of the square

SOURCE OF DESIGN   A carved stone vase from Honduras

The number of squares will depend on the size of the quilt, whether for a cot, bunk, single or double bed. If a 6″ square is taken as an average size, the embroidery line should be about ¼″ wide made up of 3 or 4 rows of stitchery. The line needs to be strong.

The simple shapes, twisted in different directions within the square grid, can also be quilted on the machine. The face could have additional hand embroidery to emphasize it and make it a focal point of the design.

A

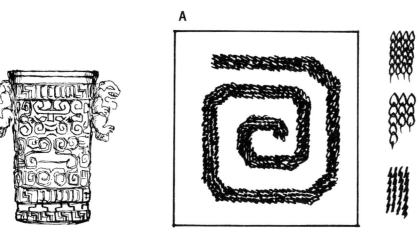

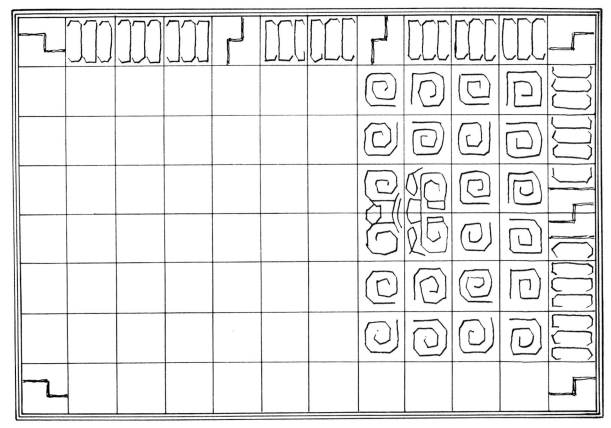

A.

B. FABRIC Good quality plain cotton for the ground; patches can be any gay color but not transparent because turnings must not show

THREAD Stranded cotton for surface stitchery
Sewing thread for hemming the patches

COLOR Any cheerful pieces that can be collected

STITCHES Satin for hands and feet
Rows of stem for arms, bird and pin on poncho
Rows of chain along edge of poncho and hem of gown
Closely worked fly for cumberbund

SOURCE OF DESIGN A painted vase in the museum at Cuzco

Such simple shapes lend themselves to appliqué. Outlines of the motif form a pattern that can be machine stitched over the center of the coverlet.

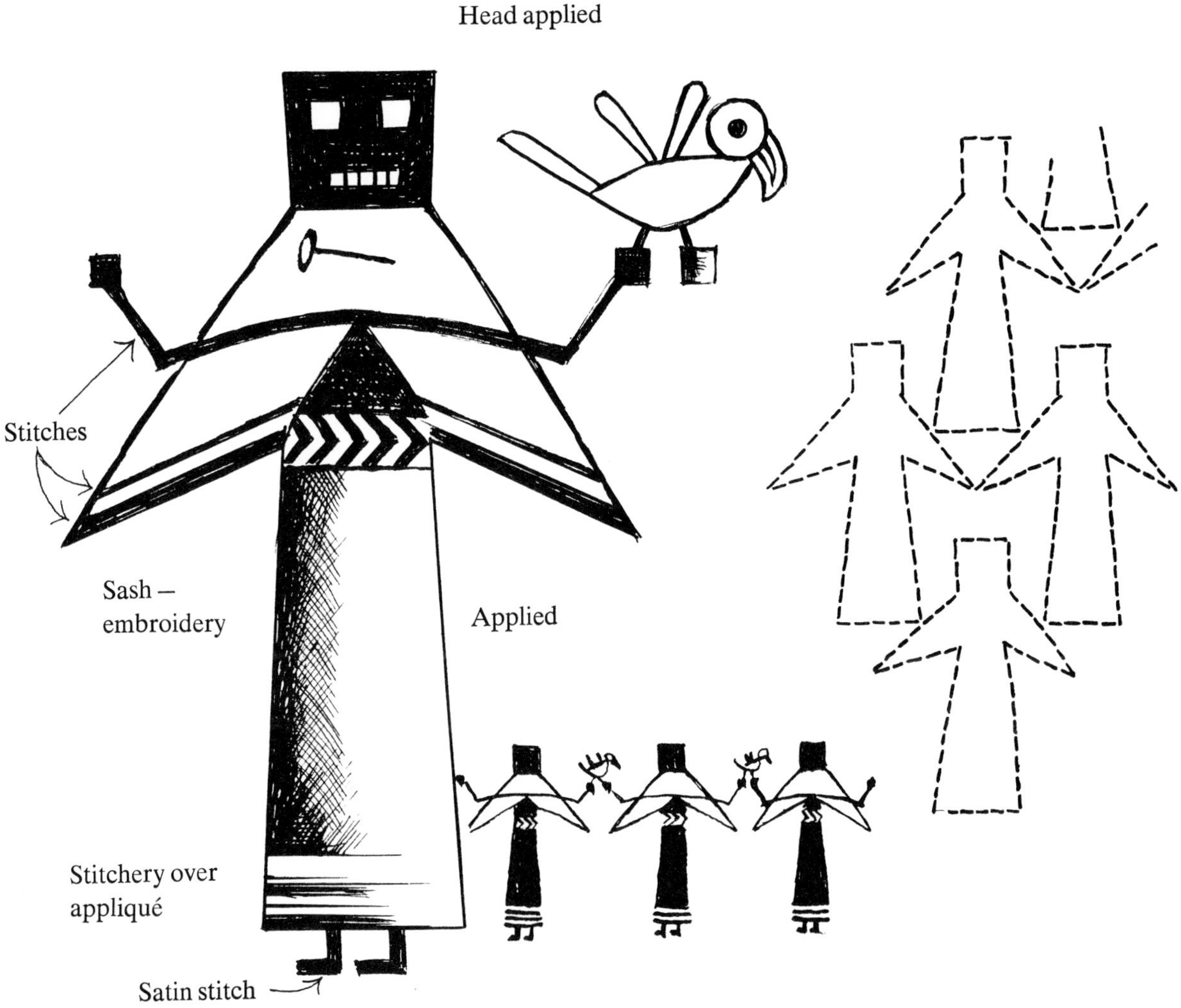

Head applied

Stitches

Sash —
embroidery

Applied

Stitchery over
appliqué

Satin stitch

B

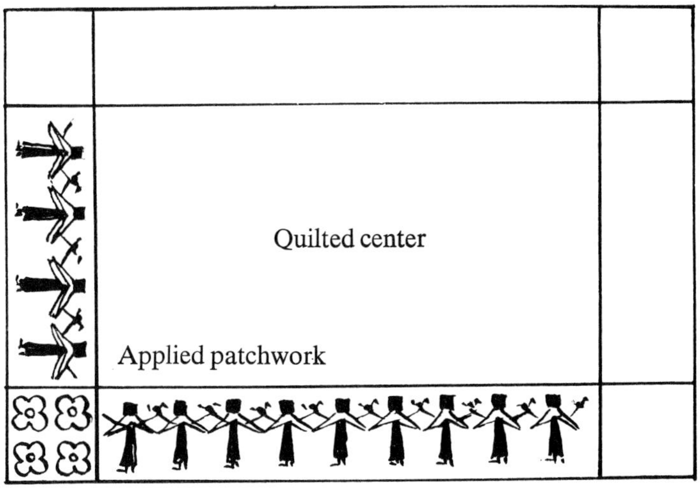

Quilted center

Applied patchwork

GEOMETRIC PATTERNS

SUITABLE FABRICS	Fine woolen curtaining, medium weight, double thread linen
THREAD	Crewel and 3 ply wool, stranded cotton
COLOR	One or two contrasting shades
STITCHES	Double running, four-sided, satin, straight, wheatsheaf, various eyelets
SOURCE OF DESIGNS	Typical patterns from Peruvian textiles and pottery
USES	Table linen, curtains

SEE PLATES 6. AND 7.

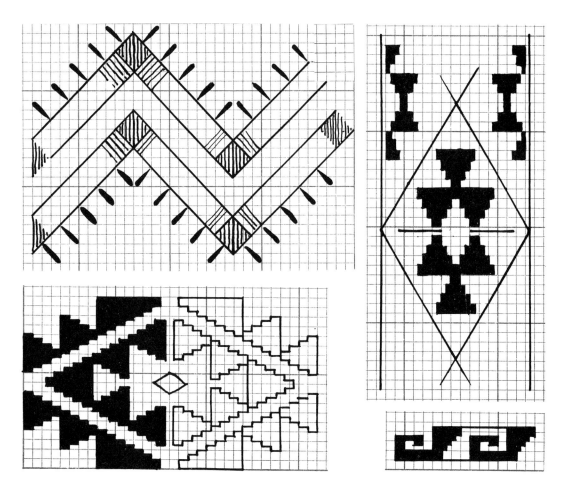

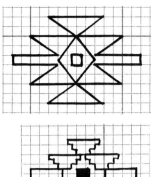

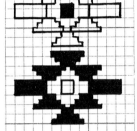

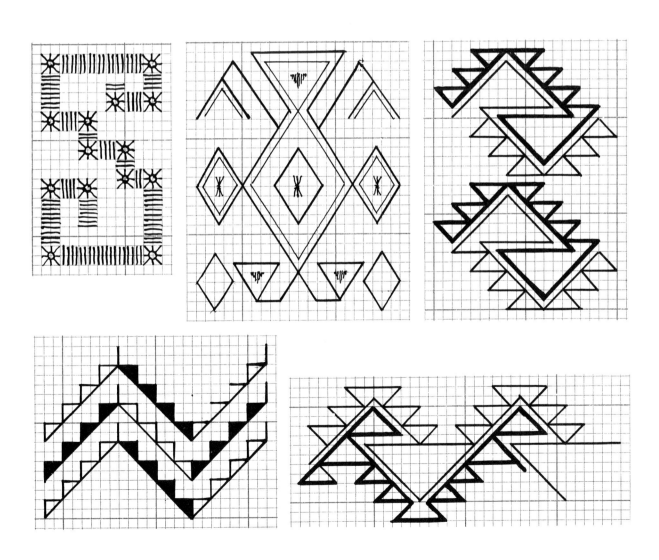

WALL PANEL/Mythical Bird

FABRIC	Red rayon, linen finish
THREAD	White pearl cotton No. 5 and No. 8
STITCHES	Chain, twisted chain, coral knot, chevron, stem, double knot, long-armed feather
SOURCE OF DESIGN	A frieze of mythical birds carved in low relief in white granite and painted black, from a temple at Chavín de Huántar, Peru.
OTHER USE	A seat cover; repeat pattern to required length

SEE PLATE 9.

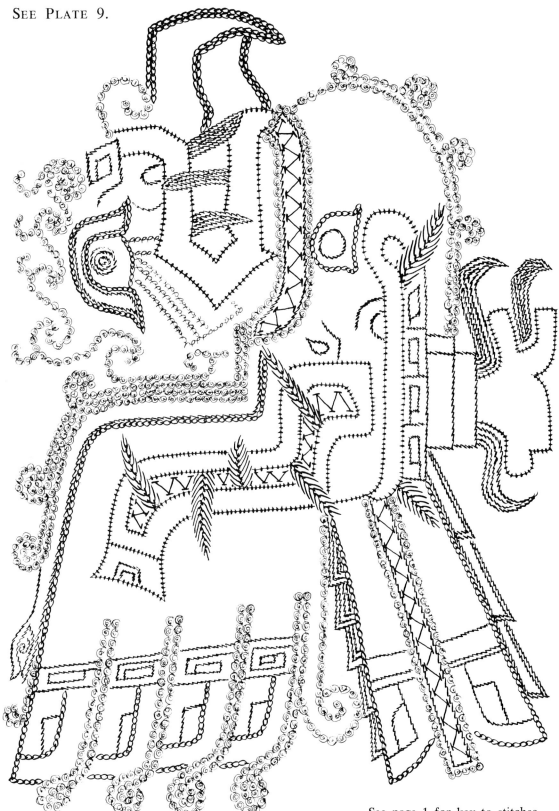

See page 1 for key to stitches.

WALL PANEL/Sea Eagle   SEE PLATE 14.

FABRIC	Slub silk
THREAD	Stranded cotton and roughly spun wool pulled from a cutting of tweed and used for couching
COLOR	*Tail:* shades from royal purple to very dark purple, royal blue for couching
	Head feathers: royal blue couching between alternate rows of purple and navy blue
	Upper wing: shades of red with purple and navy spots
	Main wing: shades of Prussian blue with yellow and green spots
	Breast: divided from wing by a black-and-white line; rays in shades of red
	Legs: purple
	Claws: pale green
	Mouth and beak: yellow
	Eye: black and white
	Bowl: brown and navy blue
	Background texture: gray
STITCHES	Back, closed herringbone, Cretan, coral knot, couching, feather, interlaced cross, satin, spider web, stem, twisted chain
SOURCE OF DESIGN	Late Mochica painted pottery

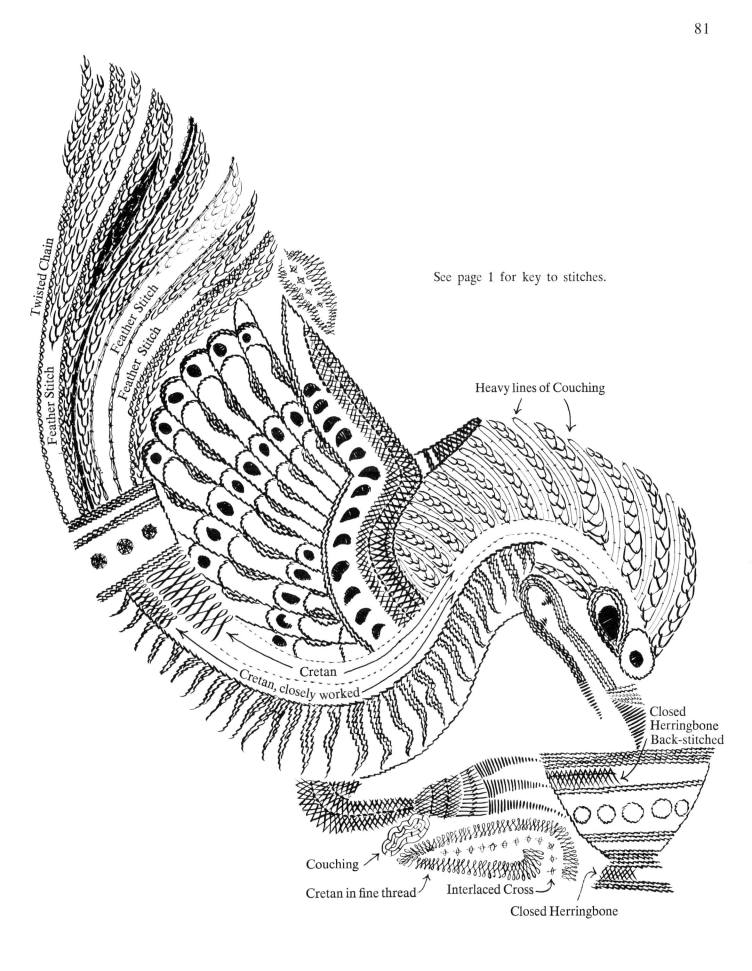

Twisted Chain

Feather Stitch

Feather Stitch

Feather Stitch

See page 1 for key to stitches.

Heavy lines of Couching

Cretan

Cretan, closely worked

Closed Herringbone Back-stitched

Couching

Cretan in fine thread

Interlaced Cross

Closed Herringbone

WALL PANEL/Dragon SEE PLATE 11.

FABRIC	Burlap, felt for appliqué
THREAD	Crewel wool, stranded cotton, coton à broder, cotton gimp
COLOR	Brown, with rusts and creams
STITCHES	Buttonhole, closed buttonhole, couching, chain, feather, French knots, spider web, tufting, stem, rosette chain
SOURCE OF DESIGN	A funerary urn from Panama that has a strange creature painted in reddish brown and outlined in black. The embroidery design is based on its tail, which turned upside down suggests a dragon.
OTHER USES	Cushion or bag

Stretch over cardboard before framing. See page 89.

See page 1 for key to stitches.

DECORATIVE PANEL OR CUSHION

SEE PLATE 1.

FABRIC	Golden burlap
THREAD	Crewel wool
COLOR	Maroon, navy dark brown, vermilion, orange, lime green, shades of yellow
STITCHES	Cross, double cross, long-armed cross, diagonal Florentine, Parisian, rice, tent, stem, wheatsheaf, woven and spider web, tufting, a few French knots
SOURCE OF DESIGN	A panel on a painted textile, probably Colombian

Either the head or the body of this strange being would make an unusual design. Here the head has been turned into a brilliantly colored wall panel but it could, without any different embroidery treatment, have been made up as a cushion. Variety in texture is important. Close flat stitches are contrasted with areas of tufting, canvas stitches are contrasted with smooth areas filled with stem stitch. Some of the golden fabric shows within the design, adding to its brightness.

Continuous row of tufts

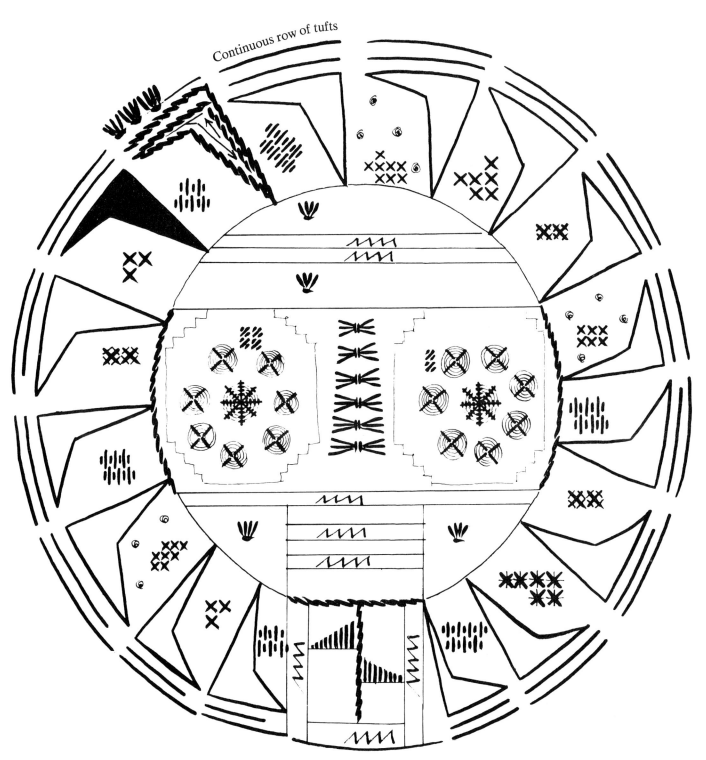

See page 1 for key to stitches.

WALL PANEL/Composite Birds

Composite birds each having two feet while sharing one body. The motif is derived from a Tiahuanaco textile. In the original mantle the outline is consistently the lightest tone. In alternate panels the background is light and dark, the panels divided by a simple geometric band.

In the cartoon the outline is not all the same width and the lines are not all parallel; this is done deliberately to avoid monotony. Embroidery can be kept entirely to these bands, or the spaces can be filled with color. One of many possible tone arrangements is suggested below, two others opposite.

OTHER USES   a. A bath mat in nylon yarn on coarse canvas

b. A seat cover in a dining alcove; repeat the pattern to required length

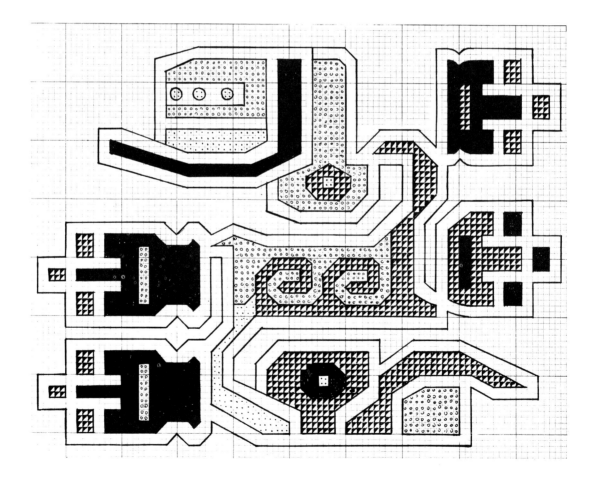

WALL PANEL/Eagle

The simple lines of this design can be worked in the same stitches as those used in the white bird. No stitchery is shown, encouraging the imaginative embroiderer to decide which feathers should be filled in, in contrast to those left in outline.

If a color treatment is preferred, use deep tones similar to those in the Sea Eagle.

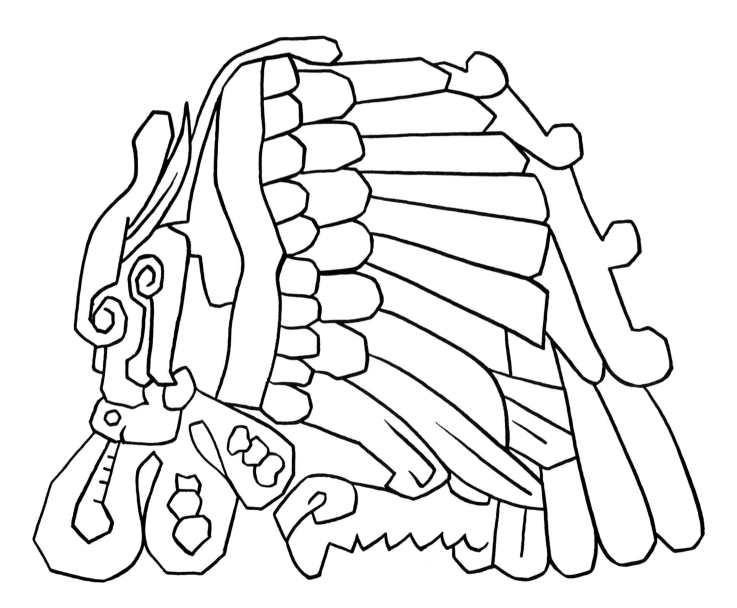

HOW TO MOUNT A PANEL

Find a piece of strong cardboard. Place the embroidery carefully over this, moving it slightly one way or the other until the margins round the design look well; generally a little more space should be left at the bottom. Pin in a few places along each side to prevent the material from slipping. Turn over, face downwards on to a clean cloth. Use a few spots of rubber-based glue along each side, pulling the material taut. Glance at the front to see that the material has not slipped. If all is well, glue down firmly, except at the corners which need to be mitered. Fold the corner of the fabric across the corner of the card, secure with a spot of glue; then bring each side across in turn, sticking carefully.

In the case of the Dragon and the Sun the mounted panels were placed on another covered card to improve the color effect.

If work is to be framed professionally it should be mounted over card with allowance made for approximately ¼″ covered by the edge of the frame.

MOUNTING HESSIAN OVER CARD

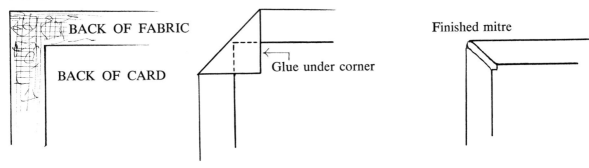

BACK OF FABRIC

BACK OF CARD

Glue under corner

Finished mitre

MOTIFS ADAPTED FOR CROSS-STITCH

Motifs taken from textiles, carved wooden implements, stone carvings, and geometric bands on pottery, adapted for cross-stitch or other work on counted threads.

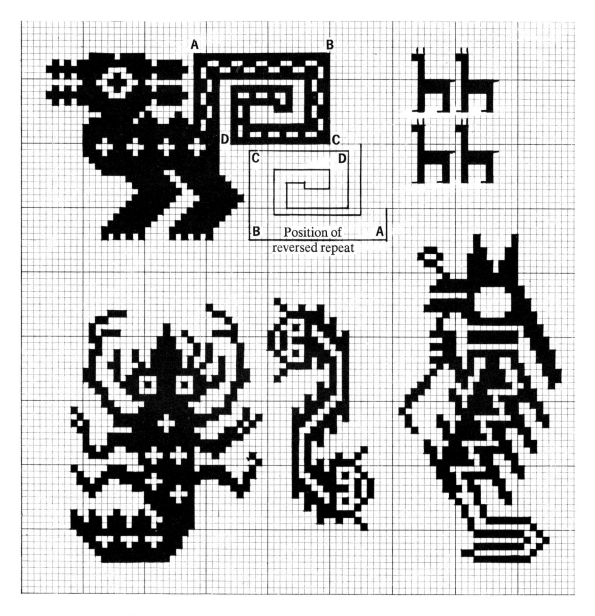

A. Puma, llama, crayfish, serpent, mouse with snake

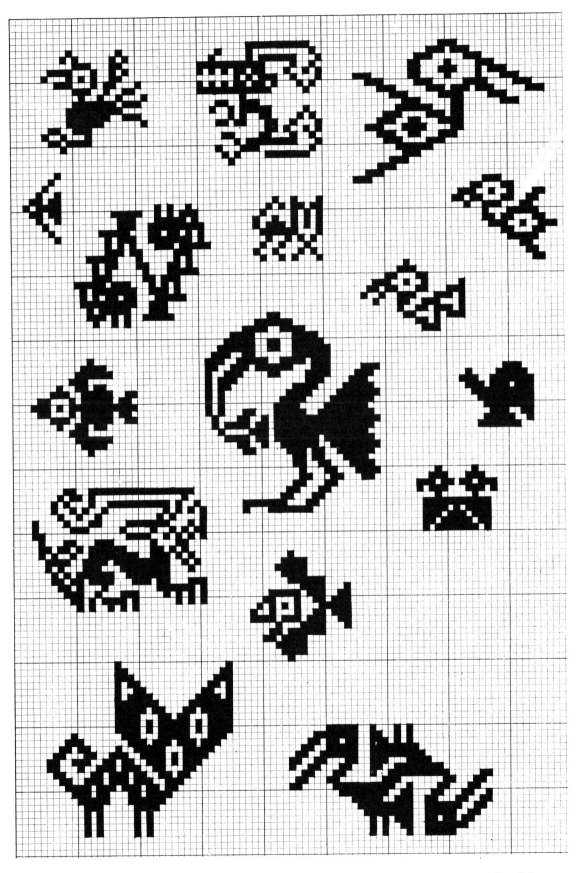

B.   Birds, with the pelican predominant, mythical creatures, two cats, and a fish

DRESS ACCESSORIES

Fashion changes rapidly. Every year the focal point is different and accessories change accordingly. For example, hems, waistlines, belts, yokes, and pockets move up and down. Ideas from the past look less ridiculous than the previous year's fashion. Embroidery on clothes should probably be worked quickly so that an idea will not be out of date before the garment has been worn.

Buy a suitable pattern and decide how to make it unique by adding a motif or border to emphasize some feature of the garment. Several motifs are suggested; their choice and treatment must depend on the use to which they are put and the fabric on which they are worked. Generally wool or stranded cotton can be used on woolen material; stranded cotton on cotton. Stranded cotton may have to be used on silk because pure silk thread is hard to find.

Consider how often the garment will be washed or whether it will always be dry-cleaned.

MOTIFS FROM VARIOUS SOURCES WITH SUGGESTIONS FOR THEIR USE

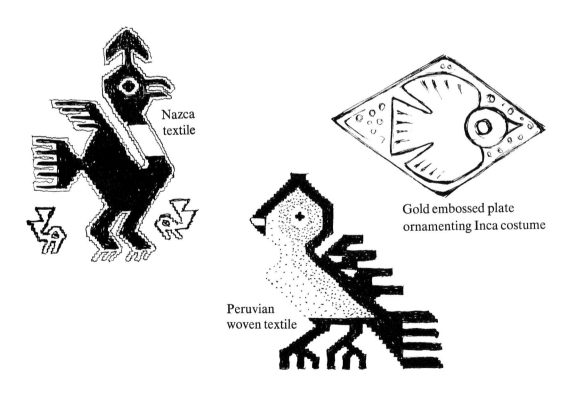

Nazca textile

Gold embossed plate ornamenting Inca costume

Peruvian woven textile

DRESS ACCENTS, ACCESSORIES

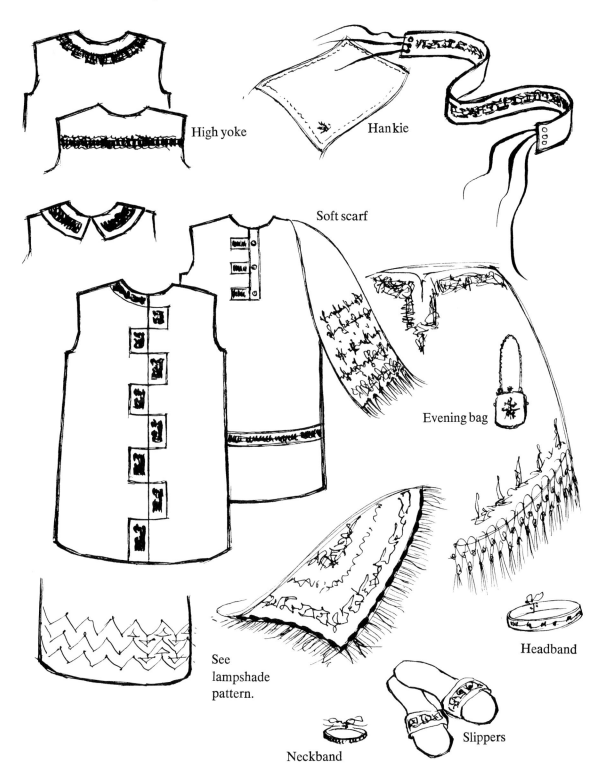

High yoke

Hankie

Soft scarf

Evening bag

See
lampshade
pattern.

Headband

Neckband

Slippers

One of a series of gold embossed ornamental plaques used to cover Inca royal clothing

From Peruvian printed textile

From gold embossed funerary glove

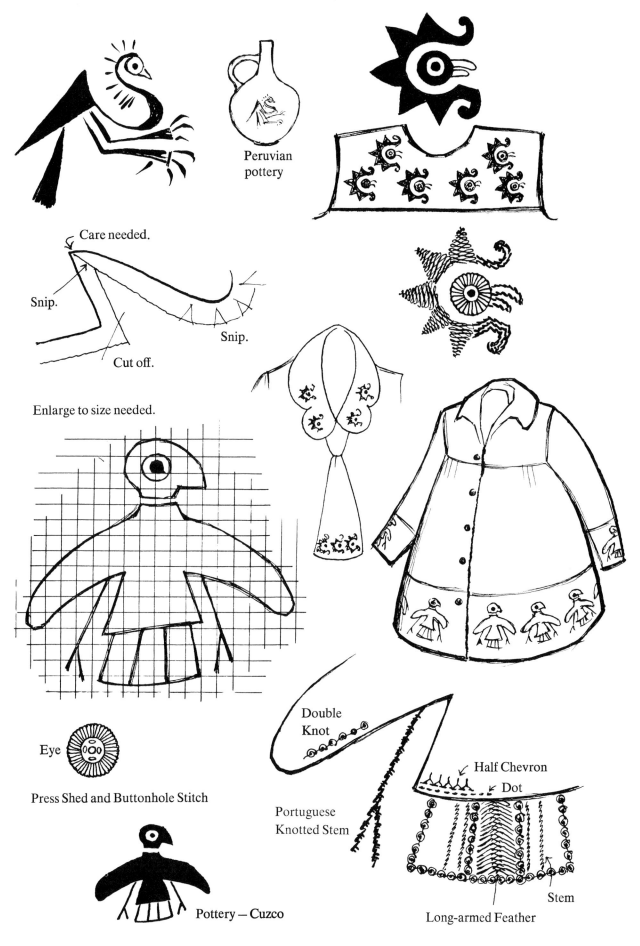

Peruvian
pottery

Care needed.

Snip.

Cut off.

Snip.

Enlarge to size needed.

Eye

Press Shed and Buttonhole Stitch

Pottery — Cuzco

Double
Knot

Half Chevron

Dot

Portuguese
Knotted Stem

Stem

Long-armed Feather

BORDER/Long Faces

SEE PLATE 4.

FABRIC	Checked cotton
THREAD	Stranded cotton, coton à broder
COLOR	Grey, mauve, royal purple, orange, yellow, gold threads on purple and cerise fabric
STITCHES	Back, chain, herringbone, closed herringbone, couching, Cretan, double knot, dot, half chevron, satin, stem
SOURCE OF DESIGN	Effigy beakers in gold and silver from the Ica Valley and coastal regions, Peru
USES	Robe, apron

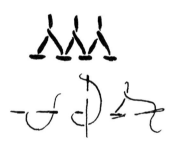

HALF CHEVRON

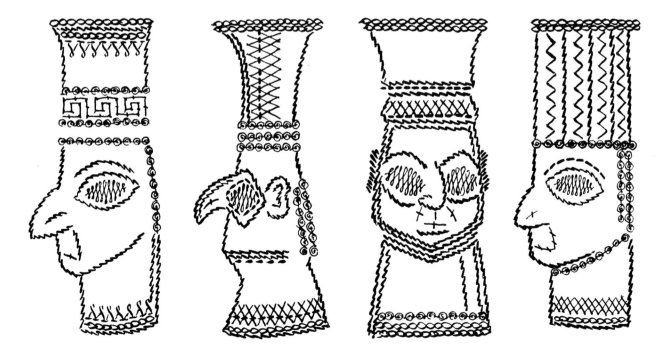

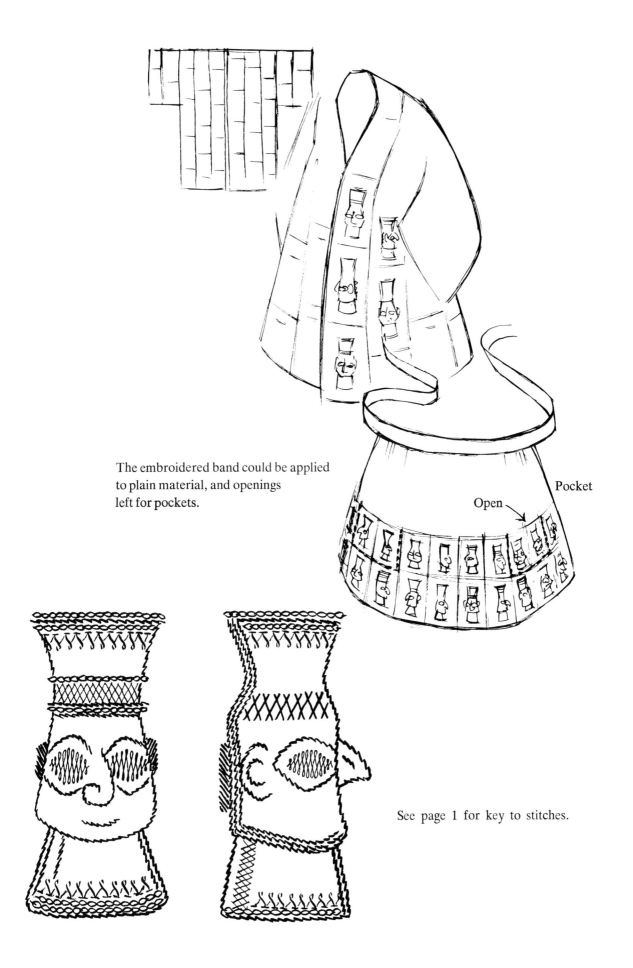

The embroidered band could be applied
to plain material, and openings
left for pockets.

Open

Pocket

See page 1 for key to stitches.

DESIGN MOTIF/Mouse

A.

FABRIC	Apricot linen and white iron-on fabric
THREAD	Stranded cotton
COLOR	Salmon outline; eyes, black and white
STITCHES	Back, buttonhole, buttonhole wheel, chain, French knots, interlaced cross, satin
SOURCE OF DESIGN	Tripod clay vessel representing a jaguar; white ground painted in black with touches of rust, Costa Rica

B.

FABRIC	Linen, 2 shades bright pink, 2 shades jade green
THREAD	Stranded cotton
COLOR	Black, white
SUGGESTED USES	a. Corner of a collar, or a lapel, or a handkerchief
	b. Yoke motifs
	c. Pocket, hat, or top of slippers
	d. Patchwork jacket
	e. Lampshade
	f. Place mat covered with Plexiglas

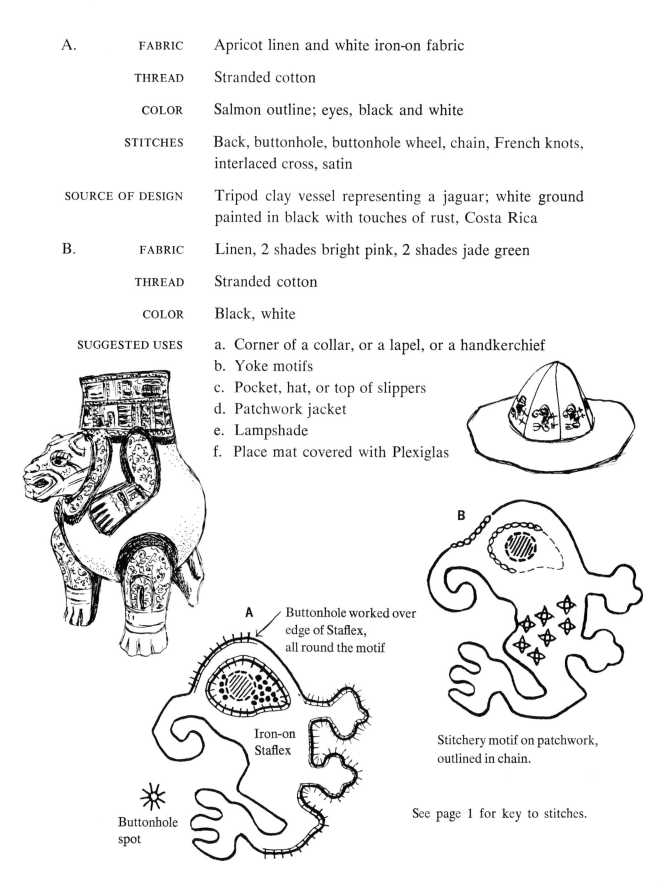

A

Buttonhole worked over edge of Staflex, all round the motif

Iron-on Staflex

Buttonhole spot

B

Stitchery motif on patchwork, outlined in chain.

See page 1 for key to stitches.

DESIGN MOTIF/Fish

SEE PLATE 3.

FABRIC	Grey and orange linen, fawn gloving leather
THREAD	Dark brown stranded cotton
STITCHES	Buttonhole, stem
SOURCE OF DESIGN	Pottery vessel representing a man, southern Peru. Off-white ground, painted mainly in dark red brown with a little rust and slightly more purplish brown, outlined in black.
SUGGESTED USES	As for Mouse, page 98.
HOW TO MAKE	Cut the whole shape in gray linen.

Cut the upper part in brown and stick to the gray along the center only; any adhesive which comes near the edge is too hard to sew through.

Work the buttonhole, then stem stitch; finally glue on leather eye.

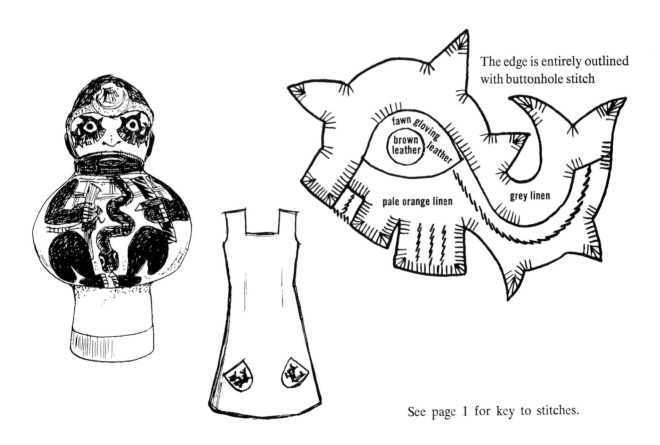

The edge is entirely outlined with buttonhole stitch

fawn gloving leather

brown leather

pale orange linen

grey linen

See page 1 for key to stitches.

DESIGN MOTIF/Birds

SOURCE OF DESIGN   A carved border on an adobe wall, Chanchan, Peru

A. Drawn in outline for Italian quilting, or trapunto. Thin, but not transparent, material is best.

Draw the design on coarse muslin. Tack this behind the top material.

Work the lines in small stem stitch through both fabrics, producing backstitch on the front.

Still working from the back, with a blunt needle thread the wool into the shapes until they are raised. To prevent puckering, leave a tiny loop each time the padding thread re-enters the muslin.

Italian quilting can decorate evening purses and slippers made of silk. If used on jackets or boleros, pad lightly; over-tight padding gives a lumpy, untidy result.

B. C. D. *Some of many possible interpretations in surface stitchery.*

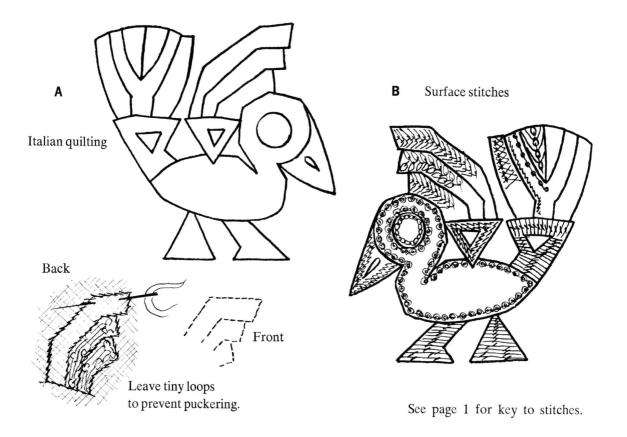

A

Italian quilting

Back

Front

Leave tiny loops
to prevent puckering.

B   Surface stitches

See page 1 for key to stitches.

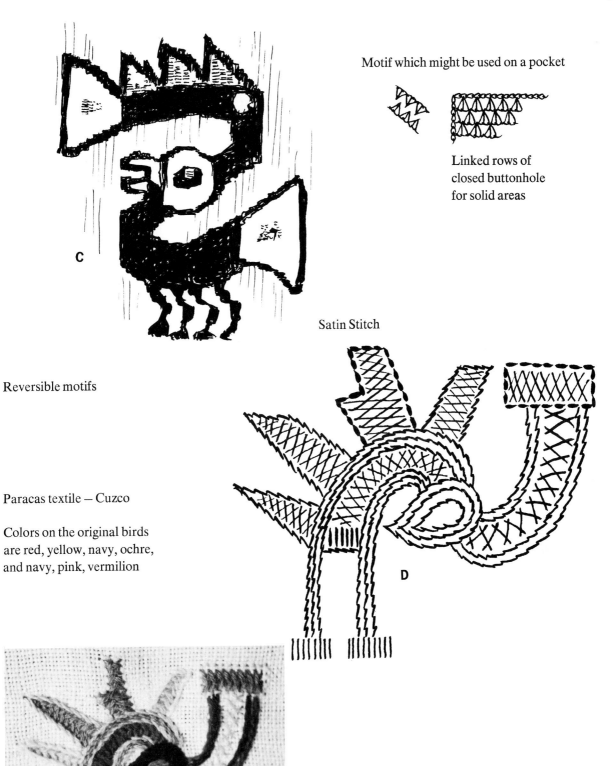

Motif which might be used on a pocket

Linked rows of
closed buttonhole
for solid areas

C

Satin Stitch

Reversible motifs

Paracas textile — Cuzco

Colors on the original birds
are red, yellow, navy, ochre,
and navy, pink, vermilion

D

See page 1 for key to stitches.

HAND TOWEL or PONCHO

SEE PLATE 16.

FABRIC   Red toweling

THREAD   Stranded cotton, pearl cotton No. 5

STITCHES   Couching

SOURCE OF DESIGN
a. One of about 200 closely packed figures, all different, on an Early Nazca printed fabric. Surface stitches are suggested for use on a casual shirt.
b. Tapestry figure wearing a plumed headdress .
c. A dark printed clay pot from Abancay, Peru.
d. Warrior with bolas from a large black cloth. All warriors were outlined in pink; the colors—mainly muted shades of yellow, dull blue, yellow green, and mauve —were arranged differently in each figure.

HOW TO MAKE A PONCHO
Fold a square of material cornerways; cut a slit to fit comfortably over the head.
Bind the neck with closely worked buttonhole stitch or bind the raw edge or turn in once and bind flat on the inside.

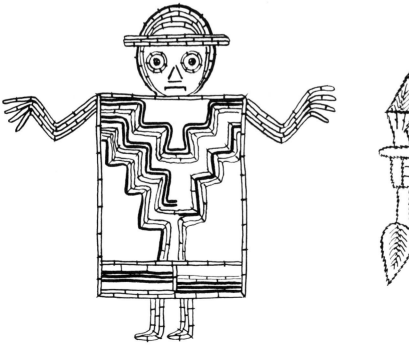

A

B

D

C

HOW TO BIND THE NECK

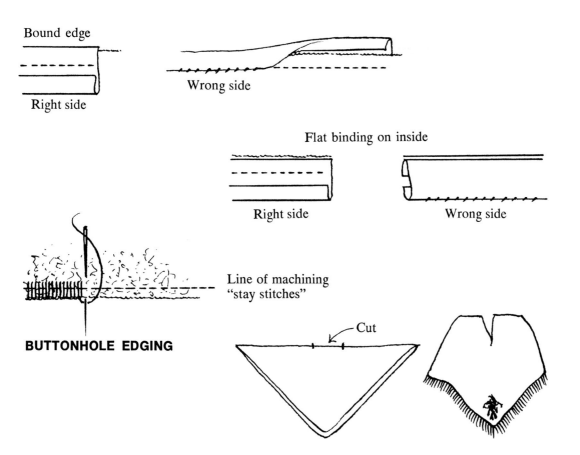

Bound edge

Right side

Wrong side

Flat binding on inside

Right side

Wrong side

Line of machining
"stay stitches"

BUTTONHOLE EDGING

Cut

SPHERICAL BAG

FABRIC	Amethyst tweed; also semi-transparent and opaque rings
THREAD	Crewel wool, sewing thread
COLOR	Seven shades of dull purple and cerise
STITCHES	Couching, French knots
SOURCE OF DESIGN	Circular patterns are often used with other geometric shapes in ceramic decoration
HOW TO MAKE	Join together two sets of three pieces to make two sides. Join the sides together, as far as X, leaving a short distance open to allow access to the bag. Sew in the hexagonal base. Line the bag after stiffening the base. Add a suitable handle.

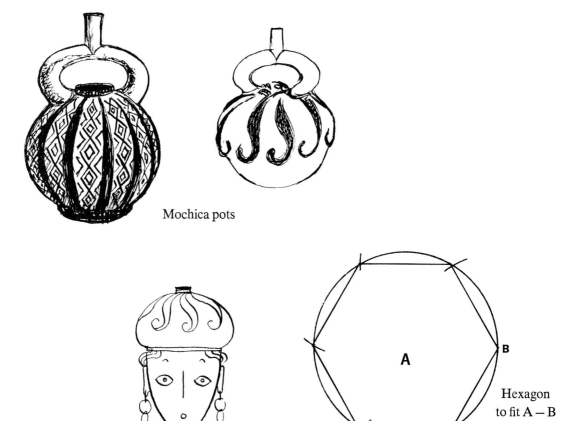

Mochica pots

Hexagon
to fit A – B

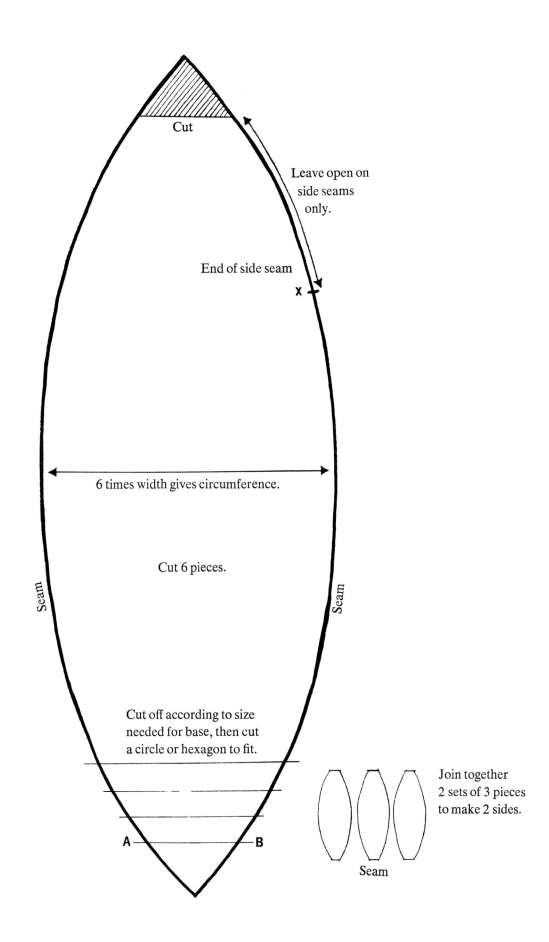

Cut

Leave open on
side seams
only.

End of side seam

x

6 times width gives circumference.

Cut 6 pieces.

Seam

Seam

Cut off according to size
needed for base, then cut
a circle or hexagon to fit.

A —— B

Join together
2 sets of 3 pieces
to make 2 sides.

Seam

BAG WITH COUNTERCHANGE DESIGN

FABRIC	Felt or blazer flannel
THREAD	Double knitting wool
COLOR	2 tones for fabric, reversed for thread
STITCHES	Double knot, coral knot, closely placed French knots
SOURCE OF DESIGN	Mochica pottery, Peru
HOW TO MAKE	Join dark and light pairs together. Line each side turning in edges and hemming to felt ¼″ from edge. Do not let stitches show on right side. Place right sides together. Machine seams. Bind opening. Sew on a pleated cord handle.

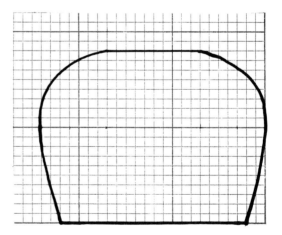

BAG WITH APPLIED DECORATION

FABRIC	Felt, 2 contrasting colors
THREAD	Crewel wool
COLOR	2 shades each of felt colors
STITCHES	Zigzag edge hemmed with matching cotton lines in alternate rows of closely worked fly and Portuguese knotted stem Circles in several rows of coral knot
SOURCE OF DESIGN	Late Paracas pottery, Peru
HOW TO MAKE	As for previous bag

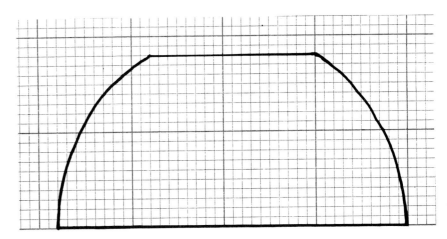

BURLAP BAG/Insect

SEE PLATE 12.

FABRIC COLOR	Dark turquoise burlap
THREAD	Crewel, tapestry wool
COLOR	Two shades of turquoise, two shades of mustard yellow, pale lime, maroon. Both wools are combined in the tassels.
STITCHES	Chain, French knots, stem, a few straight stitches
SOURCE OF DESIGN	Pottery found in Cuzco Museum
HOW TO MAKE	To make the tassel, wind wool around two pieces of card. Cut the wool between the card. Tie in bunches, leaving the tie ends long enough to sew the tassel onto the bag. Fold a bunch, wind wool around several times, tie and stab the ends through to secure them.

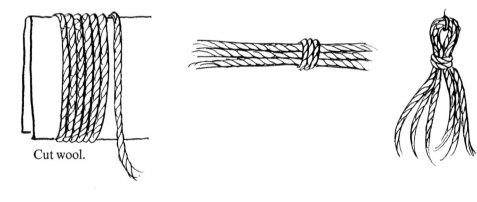

Cut wool.

BURLAP BAG/Cat

SEE PLATE 12.

FABRIC COLOR	Vermilion burlap
THREAD	Crewel wool
COLOR	Dark blue, two shades of dark turquoise, dull orange, dull slightly greenish yellow
STITCHES	Cretan, satin, stem, straight
SOURCE OF DESIGN	Cat A. Chimu textile; cat B. Paracas wool embroidery, the original worked entirely in stem stitch

Diagram to show repeat

On a pink ground, best described as medium pale "shocking" pink

ochre with some clearer yellow, but never gamboge

dark turquoise with touch ultramarine

blue repeat

yellow repeat

blue repeat

blue repeat

yellow repeat

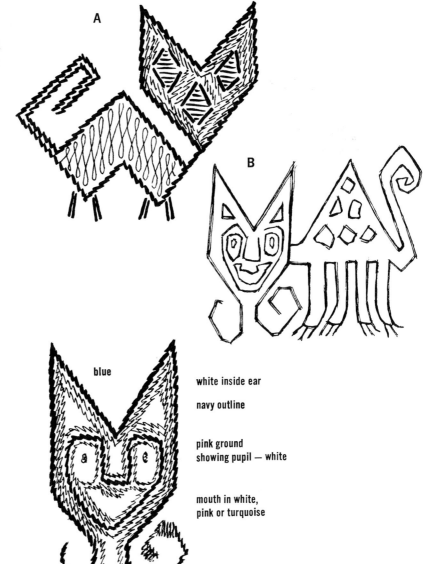

A

B

blue

white inside ear

navy outline

pink ground showing pupil — white

mouth in white, pink or turquoise

BURLAP BAG/Hummingbird

FABRIC COLOR	Midnight blue
THREAD	Crewel wool
STITCHES	Buttonhole, chain, stem, straight
COLOR	Crimson and dark red, medium and pale turquoise, dull yellow
SOURCE OF DESIGN	Hummingbirds are a recurrent theme on Nazca pottery.

3 Hessian Bags

SEE PLATE 12.

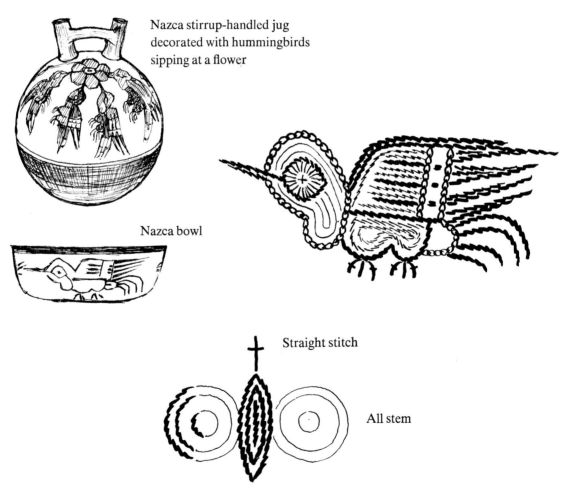

Nazca stirrup-handled jug decorated with hummingbirds sipping at a flower

Nazca bowl

Straight stitch

All stem

BAG/Llama

Llamas are a common motif on Peruvian woven pouches of the Inca period. (They are sometimes accompanied by other motifs, human beings and a strange animal or a bird, certainly not a llama because it has neither ears nor tail.)

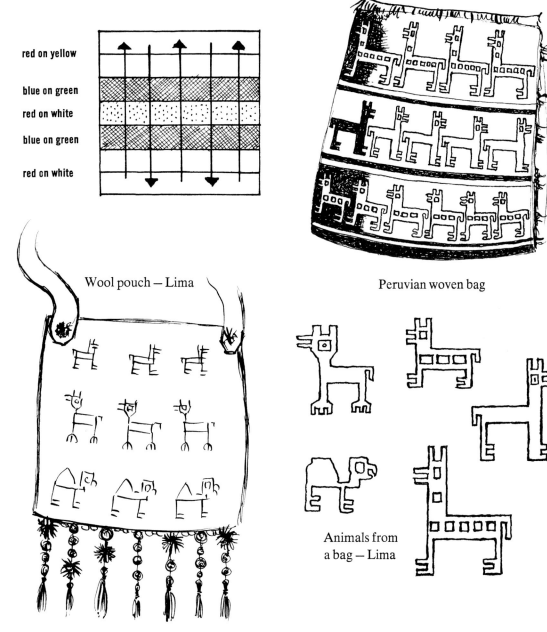

red on yellow

blue on green

red on white

blue on green

red on white

Wool pouch – Lima

Peruvian woven bag

Animals from a bag – Lima

Use large beads, pompoms and outsize tassels for a fringe.

Designs could be used for Assisi work, in which the motif is outlined with double running and the background filled in with long armed cross.

HOW TO MAKE BAG HANDLES

Cut a 4″ wide strip a comfortable length; a long handle takes the whole width of the material. Fold in to the center; tack in place; if there is a selvedge, machine to the ends, otherwise turn the ends in and sew by hand. Having already lined the bag while it is flat now mark the center of each side and the strap width. Tack the strap in place and machine from the outside; sew the end by hand.

MAKING THE HANDLE

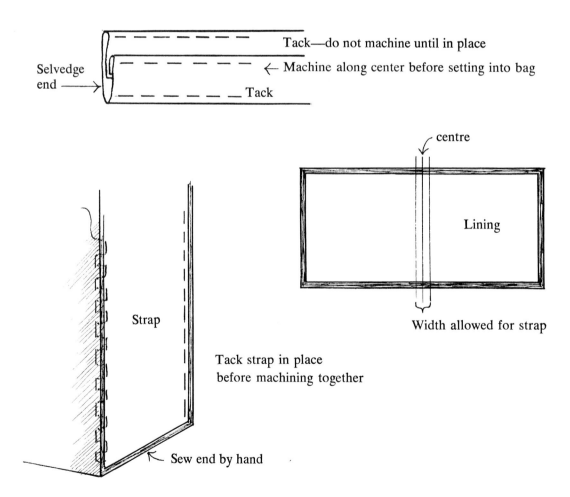

Tack—do not machine until in place

Selvedge end →

← Machine along center before setting into bag

Tack

centre

Lining

Width allowed for strap

Strap

Tack strap in place
before machining together

Sew end by hand

BAG WITH RING DECORATIONS

FABRIC	Amethyst tweed; also semi-transparent and opaque rings
THREAD	Crewel wool, sewing thread
STITCHES	Couching, French knots
COLOR	Seven shades of dull purple and cerise
SOURCE OF DESIGN	Circular patterns are often used with other geometric shapes in ceramic decoration

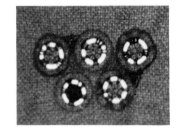

More designs for tote bags

Semi-transparent white rings

White opaque ring

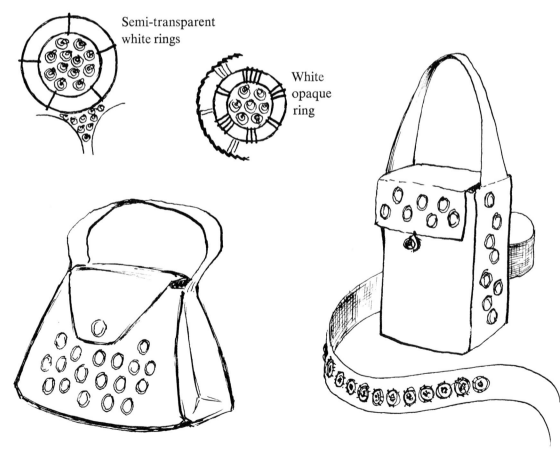

IDEAS FOR BAGS

SOURCE OF DESIGN   Based on a Mochica vase in the
Rafael Larco Hoyle Museum, Lima

Choice of material depends on what is available. Bags for beach use need a plastic lining. Any bag which is to be washed frequently should be worked in cotton.

Several ways of filling the compartments are shown. They are not necessarily intended to be used together. The proportions are varied to show how easily the design can be adapted. Once it is decided how large the bag will be, cut a paper pattern and draw the shapes on it with a colored pencil until the curves look right from every direction.

Peruvian geometric patterns are seldom absolutely accurate, but their irregularity appears to be instinctively balanced. The designs are spontaneous, never untidy.

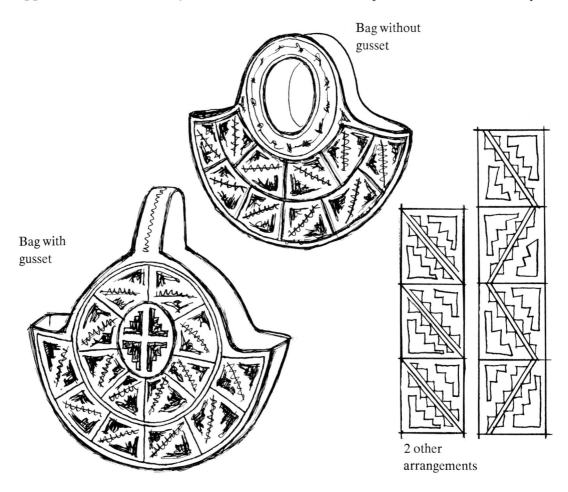

Bag without gusset

Bag with gusset

2 other arrangements

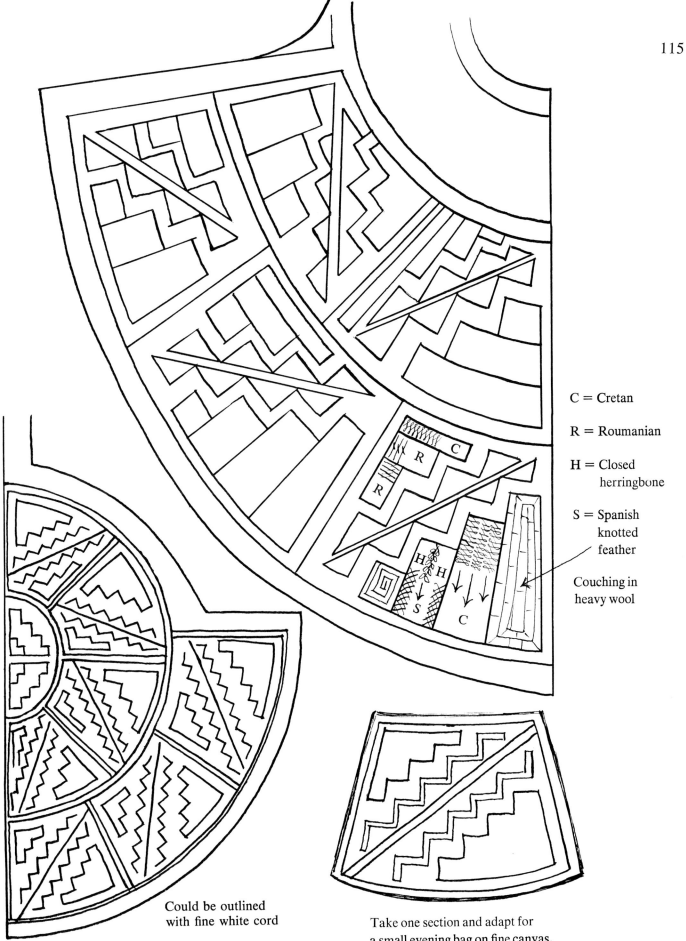

C = Cretan

R = Roumanian

H = Closed herringbone

S = Spanish knotted feather

Couching in heavy wool

Could be outlined with fine white cord

Take one section and adapt for a small evening bag on fine canvas, or a larger design on a group cushion

BELT I

FABRIC	Worsted suiting; also Russian braid (if available) and sewing thread
THREAD	Coton à broder
COLOR	A contrasting tone to fabric
STITCH	Heavy or broad chain
SOURCE OF DESIGN	A Mayan stone relief carving, Veracruz, Mexico
HOW TO MAKE	Having completed the embroidery turn back the edges and tack them down. Turn down the edges of the lining, making this slightly narrower. If the belt needs stiffening insert this between back and front before tacking them together. Hem lining on both edges. Fashions in clasps vary; whatever the choice of style, allowance should be made at each end for a buckle or other fastening.

Russian braid, though effective, is more easily managed on a design of continuous lines. The first part of the drawing shows how many ends had to be tucked under, and as each end frays unless oversewn, the process is tedious.

An alternative method, which would be easier to work and which would wear better although it is less distinctive, would be to embroider with heavy chain using a firm thread. This suggests the appearance of the braid.

RUSSIAN BRAID BELT

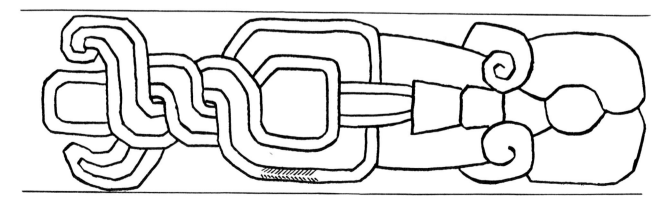

BELT II

FABRIC	White slub silk, muslin lining
THREAD	White machine embroidery thread
STITCHES	Italian quilting
SOURCE OF DESIGN	Clay vessel, Recuay style, Peru The puma-like animal would work equally well.
HOW TO MAKE	See page 116.

The design was worked originally as a napkin ring with a "touch and close" fastening for which a ¾ inch overlap was allowed. The design is suitable for an evening belt, and if not quilted, could be outlined in heavy chain or rows of Portuguese knotted stem using pearl cotton No. 5.

Animal A used for cross-stitch, see page 91.

B

TIES

SEE PLATE 13.

A.   FABRIC   White spotted tie silk

THREAD   Stranded cotton

COLOR   Red, yellow

STITCHES   Stem, back stitched spider web

SOURCE OF DESIGN   Flies on vase, page 19

B.   FABRIC   Denim, red

THREAD   Stranded cotton, red and white

STITCHES   Butterfly (a): back, double knot, French knot, interlaced cross, Portuguese knotted stem, stem, straight
Butterfly (b): couching, detached chain, double knot, Portuguese knotted stem, stem

SOURCE OF DESIGN   Jewelry from Monte Alban, Mexico

C.   FABRIC   Slub linen, yellow

THREAD   Stranded cotton, 3 shades blue, black

STITCHES   Back, chain, interlaced cross, satin, seeding, stem, spider web

SOURCE OF DESIGN   Pottery tray, Inca

This fly is on the pot, page 19.

TIE A

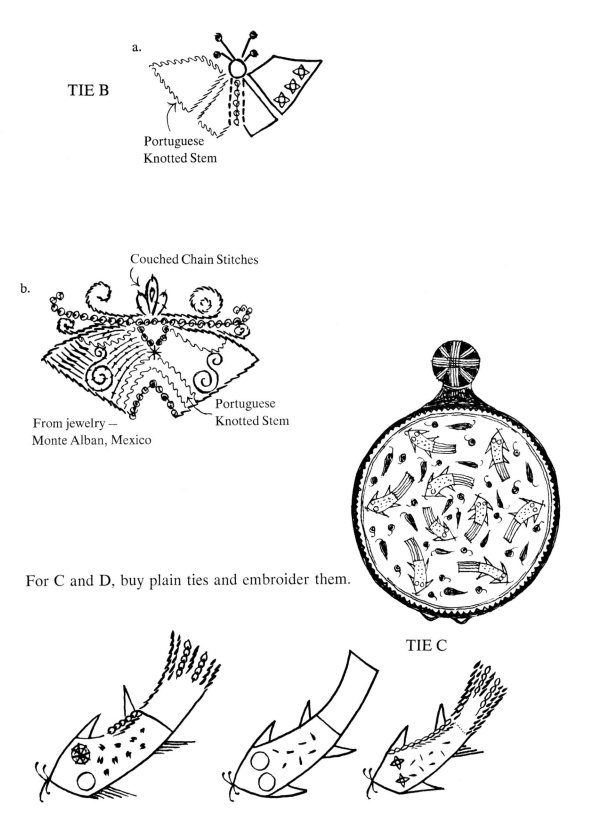

a.

TIE B

Portuguese
Knotted Stem

Couched Chain Stitches

b.

From jewelry —
Monte Alban, Mexico

Portuguese
Knotted Stem

For C and D, buy plain ties and embroider them.

TIE C

Spider web eyes

PINCUSHION

FABRIC	Dark brown worsted
THREAD	Stranded cotton, 2 shades fawn, golden yellow
STITCHES	Chain, couching
SOURCE OF DESIGN	Circular gold pectoral plate, Ecuador
HOW TO MAKE	Stuff the pincushion with animal wool or wool snippets. Do not use cotton wool or sawdust because these absorb moisture and make pins and needles rusty. Bran is the ideal substance but may now be hard to find.

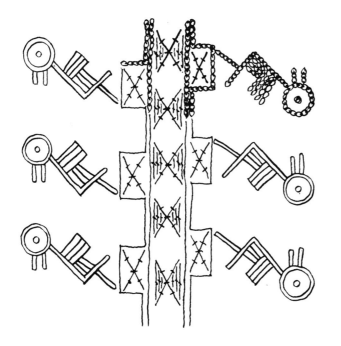

SLIPPER BAND

SEE PLATE 4.

FABRIC	Aida canvas
THREAD	Pearl cotton No. 5
STITCH	Cross
SOURCE OF DESIGN	Pottery and textiles from Peru

CONSTRUCTION OF SLIPPER WITH BAND

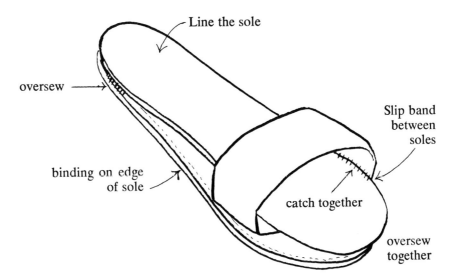

Line the sole

oversew →

binding on edge of sole →

Slip band between soles

catch together

oversew together

CROCODILE BAND

SEE PLATE 15.

FABRIC	Natural burlap
THREAD	Various wools
STITCHES	Couching, interlaced cross, satin, stem
COLOR	*Outline:* dark plum couched with purple, and salmon pink couched with yellow ochre *Inner lines:* pale greenish yellow couched with the same tint *Body:* filled with Vandyke stitch in blocks of dull purple, old gold, turquoise, pale gold, salmon, plum, royal purple, cerise, and navy
SOURCE OF DESIGN	Tapestry-weave hanging, central coast, Peru
SUGGESTED USES	a. Headband b. Belt c. In alternately facing rows on bag or cushion

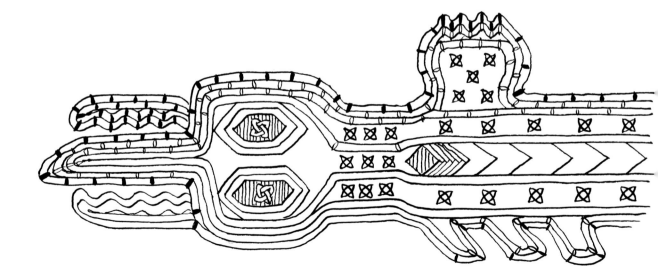

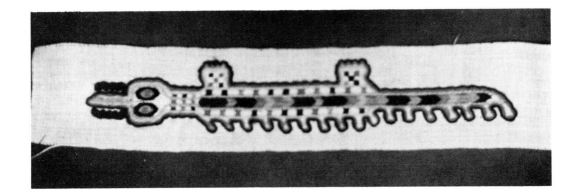

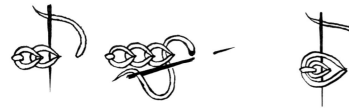

BROAD CHAIN   **HEAVY CHAIN**

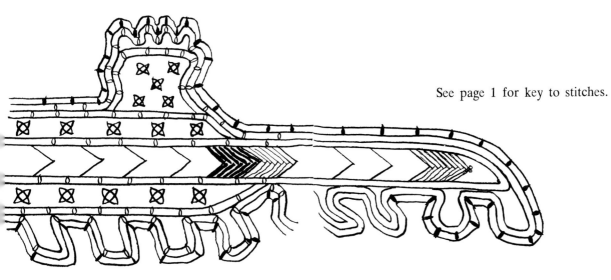

See page 1 for key to stitches.

LLAMA BAND

SEE PLATE 4.

FABRIC	Woolen tweed
THREAD	Crewel wool
COLOR	Lavender fabric; black and white wool
STITCHES	Back, satin, stem, straight
SOURCE OF DESIGN	Painted clay bowl covered with concentric rings of ornament, Peru
SUGGESTED USES	a. Any band emphasizing the design of a garment
	b. Repeated in alternate rows on a tote bag

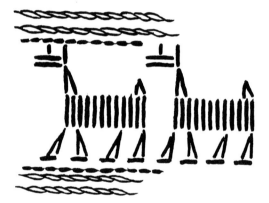

Repeat arrangements
showing direction   or

BORDER DESIGN

FABRIC	Terra cotta linen
THREAD	Black and white stranded cotton, coton à broder
STITCHES	Chain, twisted chain, double knot, French knot, stem
SOURCE OF DESIGN	Inca pottery, Pachacamac, Peru
SUGGESTED USES	a. To emphasize the edge of a yoke or waistline b. On a cuff or belt c. Guitar strap

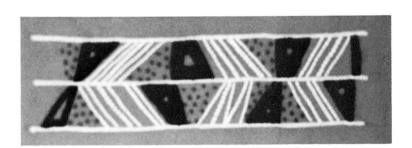

See page 1 for key to stitches.

Closely filled with stem

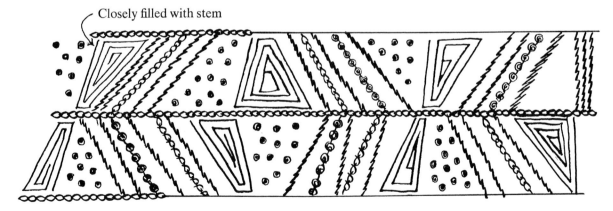

BORDER DESIGN

FABRIC	Brown worsted
THREAD	Stranded cotton, bouclé yarn
COLOR	Grey, pale jade green, light brown
STITCHES	Chain, couching, satin, stem
SOURCE OF DESIGN	Pottery vessel, Mochica
SUGGESTED USES	a. Yoke accent
	b. Buttonhole accent
	c. Belt, slipper band, headband, guitar strap
	d. Lampshade border
	e. End borders on place mats

Outlined in chain stitch,
filled with stem and satin

Couching

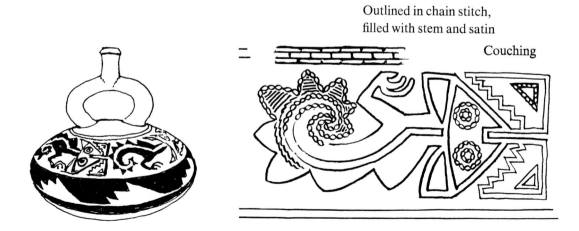

DESIGN MOTIF/Cat

SEE PLATE 3.

FABRIC	Dark brown worsted suiting
THREAD	Mohair wool, crewel wool, coton à broder
STITCHES	Couching, detached overcast, fly, Roumanian, stem; mohair wool couched with buttonhole stitch
SOURCE OF DESIGN	Suggested by a cat inside a pottery bowl, Paracas Cavernas
SUGGESTED USES	a. Wool on woolen for a dress or a poncho
	b. Hemmed appliqué in cotton or linen on clothes or a bedcover
	c. An iron-on motif with the body pattern pierced

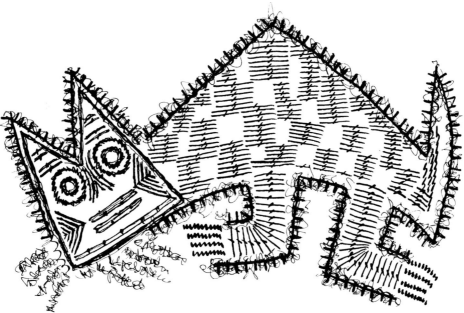

DESIGN MOTIF/Headdress

SOURCE OF DESIGN   From a headdress worn by a figure on a ceremonial axe, Chimu

SUGGESTED USES   Belts, sash ends, slippers, bags, cushions

The pattern can be worked this size, in fine thread. If enlarged, the same stitches can be used, provided they are embroidered with thicker thread. If greatly enlarged, more rows of stitchery will have to be added, rather than more rows of the pattern.

These two pages contain a rich collection of motifs which can be separated and rearranged or used in their original order. Great benefit is derived from the plain line between rows of motifs because it separates those which are completely different in shape, and it can be worked in a contrasting tone. These lines unite the whole design.

Several ways of treating the patterns are shown. Select those which are most appropriate to the use, fabric and thread chosen. Although the gold and turquoise headdress is semicircular the borders will look equally well if worked in straight lines.

Double Knot
Stem
Chain
Satin
Double Knot
Back
Satin
Stem
Double Knot
French Knots set round a bead
Double Knot

White interlining used to raise satin stitch

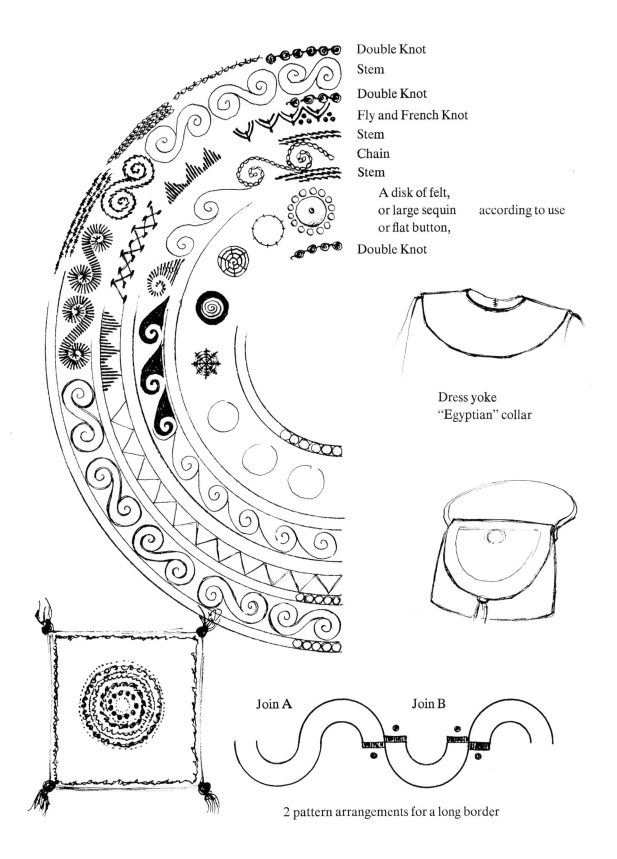

Double Knot
Stem

Double Knot
Fly and French Knot
Stem
Chain
Stem

A disk of felt,
or large sequin   according to use
or flat button,

Double Knot

Dress yoke
"Egyptian" collar

Join A   Join B

2 pattern arrangements for a long border

SPOT PATTERNS

The scattered spot motifs on page 61 suggested for use on the organdy tray-cloth will make neat border patterns when they are set close together.
Diagrams show how to bring variety into the arrangement of motifs.

Contrast: dark and light
          large and small
          solid and outline
          plain and pattern

The little dragon below, from a piece of pottery, worked in Cretan, stem, chain and satin, could be used alternately, dark and light, as a border design.

Designs on the opposite page have been selected because they are easily translated into stitchery and can be used as alternative decoration on several articles already seen in this book.

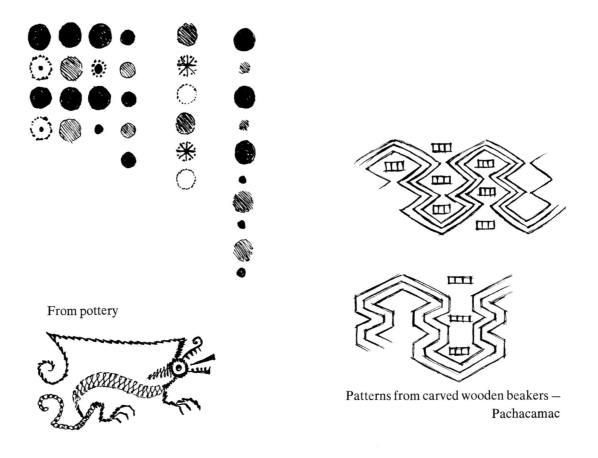

From pottery

Patterns from carved wooden beakers —
Pachacamac

A PAGE OF
GEOMETRIC PATTERNS

A — Stitchery
B — Couched
    Ring
C — Couched
    Thread

Adaptation of geometric patterns
on double spouted bottle
Lambayeque — Chimu style

Based on a gold ear-plug,
Inlaid with turquoise — Peru

The design could be used
for canvas embroidery,
applied felt, surface stitchery,
drawn fabric.

Patterns from gold funerary gloves — Chimu

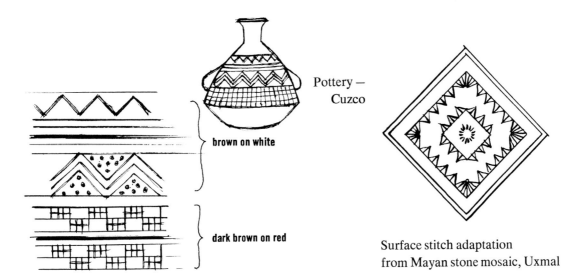

Pottery —
Cuzco

brown on white

dark brown on red

Surface stitch adaptation
from Mayan stone mosaic, Uxmal

COLOR SCHEMES

POTTERY

1. Chocolate, terracotta, ochre, grey on black ground
2. White, grey, rust, ochre
3. Terracotta, black, ochre, white
4. Dark grey, cream, rust, black, dull yellow
5. Cream, brown, rust, gold

These are some of the variations possible within a narrow range.

TEXTILES

1. Magenta, cerise or shocking pink, navy, dark turquoise, pale pink and a touch of lime
2. Orange, brown, ochre, cream, pink, turquoise
3. Deep plum, ochre, pink and navy
4. Midnight blue, magenta, plum, dull cream
5. Soft royal blue, a little pale blue, various shades of dull yellow, brown, dark brown, rusty pink, dull pea green, white
6. Dark chocolate background with shades of turquoise, pink, plum, royal blue, pale and golden yellows
7. Navy ground with dull fawn, rust and orange
8. Fawn, plum, pink, white, pale blue
9. Black, turquoise, shades of gold and orange
10. Fawn, cream, chocolate, pink, white, blue accents

There are nearly 200 shades in the Paracas dye range.

BIBLIOGRAPHY

F. ANTON & F. J. DOCKSTADER, *Pre-Columbian Art,* Abrams

H. BAUMANN, *Gold and Gods of Peru,* Oxford University Press

C. BURLAND, *The People of the Ancient Americas,* Hamlyn

G. H. S. BUSHNELL, *Ancient Arts of the Americas,* Thames and Hudson

E. O. CHRISTENSEN, *Primitive Art,* Studio-Crowell

H. D. DISSELHOFT & S. LINNÉ, *Ancient America,* Methuen

V. W. VON HAGEN, *The Ancient Sun Kingdoms of the Americas,* Thames and Hudson

RAFAEL LARCO HOYLE, *Las Epocas Pernanas,* Lima

RAFAEL LARCO HOYLE, *Archaeologia Mundi, Peru,* World Publishing Co.

R. HUYGHE, *Encyclopedia of Prehistoric and Ancient Art,* Hamlyn

J. JONES, *Art of Empire, The Inca of Peru,* The Museum of Primitive Art

M. E. KING, *Ancient Textiles from the Collection of the Textile Museum, Washington, D.C., and the Museum of Primitive Art, New York,* The Museum of Primitive Art

MONTI, *Pre-Columbian Terracottas,* Hamlyn

A. R. SAWYER, *Ancient Peruvian Ceramics,* Metropolitan Museum

A. R. SAWYER, *Mastercraftsmen of Peru,* The Solomon R. Guggenheim Foundation

EDITORS OF LIFE, *The Epic of Man,* Time Inc., N.Y.

INDEX OF STITCHES

LIST OF MUSEUMS

GREAT BRITAIN AND EUROPE

British Museum, London
National Museet, Copenhagen
Statens Ethnografiska Museum,
 Stockholm
Musée de l'Homme, Paris
Linden Museum, Stuttgart
Reitberg Museum, Zurich
Museum für Volkerkunde Vienna,
 Munich and Berlin

CENTRAL AND SOUTH AMERICA

Collection Fritz Buck, La Paz, Bolivia
*Gold Museum of the Banco de la
 Republica,* Bogota, Colombia
Museo Nacional de Antropologia,
 Mexico D.F., Mexico
Museo Regional, Oaxaca, Mexico
Museo Regional de Jalapa, Vera Cruz,
 Mexico
Museums in Costa Rica, Guatemala,
 and San Salvador
Museo Arqueologico, Cuzco, Peru
*National Museum of Anthropology
 and Archaeology,* Lima, Peru

*National Museum of History and Cul-
 ture,* Lima, Peru
Rafael Larco Herrera Museum, Lima,
 Peru
Collection Miguel Mujica Gallo, Lima
 Peru

UNITED STATES

Art Institute of Chicago
Nathan Cummings Collection, Chicago
Brooklyn Museum, New York
Metropolitan Museum, New York
Museum of the American Indian, New
 York
Museum of Primitive Art, New York
American Museum of Natural History,
 New York
Dumbarton Oaks, Washington, D.C.
National Gallery, Washington, D.C.
Smithsonian Institution, Washington,
 D.C.
Textile Museum, Washington, D.C.
 and New York
And most major cities including Bos-
 ton, Cleveland, Philadelphia, Santa
 Fe and San Francisco

LIST OF SUPPLIERS

CANADA

Harmony Acres Studio, RR1 G9 B7,
 St. Norbert, Manitoba

UNITED STATES

Appleton Bros. of London, West Main
 Road, Little Compton, Rhode Is.
 02837

The Needlecraft Shop, 4501 Van Nuys
 Blvd., Sherman Oaks, Calif. 91403
Merribee Co., Box 9680, Fort Worth,
 Texas 76107
Herrschners Needlecrafts, 72 E. Ran-
 dolph St., Chicago, Ill. 60601
Joan Toggitt, Inc., 1170 Broadway,
 New York, N.Y. 10011